WORLD BANK LATIN AMERICAN AND CARIBBEAN STUDIES

Viewpoints

Determinants of Crime Rates in Latin America and the World

An Empirical Assessment

Pablo Fajnzylber
Daniel Lederman
Norman Loayza

The World Bank
Washington, D.C.

First printing October 1998

This publication is part of the World Bank Latin American and Caribbean Studies series. Although these publications do not represent World Bank policy, they are intended to be thought-provoking and worthy of discussion, and they are designed to open a dialogue to explore creative solutions to pressing problems. Comments on this paper are welcome and will be published on the LAC Home Page, which is part of the World Bank's site on the World Wide Web. Please send comments via e-mail to laffairs@worldbank.org or via post to LAC External Affairs, The World Bank, 1818 H Street, N.W., Washington, D.C. 20433, U.S.A.

The painting on the cover, *Paracutin*, by Diego Rivera, was provided by Christie's Images.

Pablo Fajnzylber, Daniel Lederman, and Norman Loayza are economists for the World Bank's Office of the Chief Economist for Latin America and the Caribbean. Norman Loayza is also an economist for the World Bank's Development Research Group.

Library of Congress Cataloging-in-Publication Data

Fajnzylber, Pablo.
Determinants of crime rates in Latin America and the world : an empirical assessment / Pablo Fajnzylber, Daniel Lederman, and Norman Loayza.
p. cm. — (World Bank Latin American and Caribbean studies. Viewpoints)
Includes bibliographical references.
ISBN 0-8213-4240-1
1. Crime—Econometric models. 2. Crime—Latin America—Econometric models. 3. Criminal statistics. 4. Criminal statistics—Latin America. I. Lederman, Daniel, 1968– II. Loayza, Norman. III. Title. IV. Series.
HV6251.F34 1998
364.2—dc21 98-23528
CIP

CONTENTS

BOX

ACKNOWLEDGMENTS

We have benefitted from the comments and suggestions provided by Robert Barro, William Easterly, José A. González, Norman Hicks, Aart Kraay, Saul Lizondo, William Maloney, Guillermo Perry, Martin Ravallion, Luis Servén, Andrei Shleifer, Jakob Svensson, and participants at seminars in the 1997 LACEA Meetings, United Nations-ECLAC, Catholic University of Chile, the 1997 Mid-Western Macro Conference, and seminars at the World Bank. We are indebted to Lin Liu and Conrado García-Corado for research assistance. The opinions (and errors) expressed in this paper belong to the authors and do not necessarily represent the views of the World Bank, its Board of Directors, or the countries which it represents.

SUMMARY

This study uses a new data set of crime rates for a large sample of countries for the period 1970–1994, based on information from the United Nations World Crime Surveys, to analyze the determinants of national homicide and robbery rates. A simple model of the incentives to commit crimes is proposed, which explicitly considers possible causes of the persistence of crime over time (criminal inertia). Several econometric models are estimated, attempting to capture the determinants of crime rates across countries and over time. The empirical models are first run for cross-sections and then applied to panel data. The former focus on explanatory variables that do not change markedly over time, while the panel data techniques consider both the effect of the business cycle (i.e., GDP growth rate) on the crime rate and criminal inertia (accounted for by the inclusion of the lagged crime rate as an explanatory variable). The panel data techniques also consider country-specific effects, the joint endogeneity of some of the explanatory variables, and the existence of some types of measurement errors afflicting the crime data. The results show that increases in income inequality raise crime rates, deterrence effects are significant, crime tends to be counter-cyclical, and criminal inertia is significant even after controlling for other potential determinants of homicide and robbery rates.

INTRODUCTION

A GROWING CONCERN ACROSS THE WORLD is the heightened incidence of criminal and violent behavior. Rampant criminal behavior is a major concern in a variety of countries, ranging from the United States to the so-called transition economies of Eastern Europe and the developing countries in Sub-Saharan Africa and Latin America and the Caribbean.[1] A recent paper on the topic states that, "Crime and violence have emerged in recent years as major obstacles to the realization of development objectives in the countries of Latin America and the Caribbean" (World Bank 1997, abstract). In fact, crime rates for the world as a whole have been rising since the mid-1970s, as illustrated in Figure 1.

The growing public awareness is justified because rampant crime and violence may have pernicious effects on economic activity and, more generally, because they directly reduce the quality of life of all citizens who must cope with the reduced sense of personal and proprietary security. Despite the fact that violent crime is emerging as a priority in national policy agendas worldwide, we actually do not know what are the economic, social, institutional, and cultural factors thatmake some countries have higher crime rates than others over time.

At least since the publication of Becker (1968), the economics profession has analyzed the determinants of criminal behavior from theoretical and empirical points of view. Most empirical studies have addressed the issues associated with criminal behavior within cities and across regions within countries, especially the United States; yet very few empirical studies have addressed the question of why crime rates vary across countries and over time. This paper is an attempt to fill this vacuum in the economics literature.

We assembled a new data set of crime rates for a large sample of countries for the period 1970–94, based on information from the United Nations World Crime Surveys. Then, we propose a simple model of the incentives faced by individuals to commit crimes, and explicitly consider possible causes of the persistence of crime over time (criminal inertia). The empirical implementation of the model estimates several econometric models attempting to capture the determinants of crime rates across countries and over time. The empirical models are first run for cross-sections and then applied to panel data. Working with panel data (that is, pooled cross-country and time-series data) allows us to consider both the effect of the business cycle (i.e., GDP growth rate) on the crime rate and the presence of criminal inertia (accounted for by the inclusion of the lagged crime rate as an explanatory variable). Furthermore, the use of panel data techniques will allow us to account for unobserved country-specific effects, for the likely joint endogeneity of some of the explanatory variables, and for the existence of some types of measurement errors afflicting the data of reported crimes.

Some of the interesting results are the following: Greater inequality is associated with higher intentional homicide and robbery rates, but the level of income per capita is not a significant determinant of national crime rates. "Deterrence" effects are also shown to be significant. Contrary to our expectations, national enrollment rates in secondary education and the average number of years of schooling of the population appear to be positively (but weakly) associated with higher homicide rates. We address this puzzle (also found in other empirical studies) when the regression results are presented. Drug production and drug possession are both significantly associated with higher crime rates. Regarding dynamic effects, we find that the homicide rate rises during periods of low economic activity. Also, we find that crime tends to persist over time (criminal inertia), even after controlling for other determinants of criminal behavior. All these results are robust to models that take into account the likely joint endogeneity of the explanatory variables, the presence of country-specific effects, and certain types of measurement errors in reported crime rates.

The rest of the paper is organized as follows. Section II provides a selective review of theoretical and empirical contributions to the economics literature dealing with criminal behavior. Section III presents a simple economic model of criminal behavior that begins with an individual-level analysis of the incentives to commit crimes, and then considers time effects. Under a couple of assumptions, the model provides a framework to analyze the empirical determinants of national crime rates. Section IV presents the data sets used in the econometric estimation, describing the sources of the data as well as its basic statistical characteristics. Section V presents the econometric models used for estimating the impact of selected variables on national crime rates, and interprets the results of each econometric exercise. Section VI presents the conclusions of the paper and suggests future directions for research.

II LITERATURE REVIEW

IN HIS NOBEL LECTURE, Becker (1993, 390) emphasized that the economic way of looking at human behavior "implie[s] that some individuals become criminals because of the financial and other rewards from crime compared to legal work, taking account of the likelihood of apprehension and conviction, and the severity of punishment." More recent literature has emphasized the role of time effects and criminal inertia that may result from social interactions, or delayed responses to surges in criminal activity on the part of police and judicial systems.

The theoretical and empirical literature has considered the role of three types of economic conditions in determining the incidence of criminal activity, namely the average income of the communities involved, the pattern of income distribution, and the level of education. Fleisher (1966) was a pioneer in studying the role of income on the decision to commit criminal acts by individuals, and stated that the "principal theoretical reason for believing that low income increases the tendency to commit crime is that...the probable cost of getting caught is relatively low...because [low-income individuals] view their legitimate lifetime earning prospects dismally they may expect to lose relatively little earning potential by acquiring criminal records; furthermore, if legitimate earnings are low, the opportunity cost of time actually spent in delinquent activity, or in jail, is also low" (Fleisher 1966, 120). However, the level of legal income expected by an individual is not the only relevant "income" factor; the income level of potential victims also matters. The higher the level of income of potential victims, the higher the incentive to commit crimes, especially crimes against property. Thus, according to Fleisher (1966, 121), "[average] income has two conceptual influences on delinquency which operate in opposite directions, although they are not necessarily equal in strength."

Fleisher's (1966, 128–129) econometric results showed that higher average family incomes across 101 U.S. cities in 1960 were actually associated with lower court appearances by young males, and with lower numbers of arrests of young males for the crimes of robbery, burglary, larceny, and auto theft. [2] The author also found that the difference between the average income of the second lowest quartile and the highest quartile of households tended to increase city arrest and court-appearance rates, but the coefficient was often small in magnitude, and became statistically insignificant when the regressions were run for high-income communities alone.

The effects of income levels and distribution on crime were further analyzed by Ehrlich (1973, 538–540). He argued that payoffs to crime, especially property crime, depend primarily on the "opportunities provided by potential victims of crime," as measured by the median income of the families in a given community. The author assumed that, "the mean legitimate opportunities available to potential offenders," may be approximated by, "the mean income level of those below the state's median [income]" (p. 539). For a given median income, income inequality can be an indication of the differential between the payoffs of legal and illegal activities. In his econometric analysis of the determinants of state crime rates in the U.S. in 1960, Ehrlich (1973, 546–551) found that higher median family incomes were associated with higher rates of murder, rape, and assault, and with higher rates of property crimes, such as burglary. In addition, a measure of income inequality—the percentage of families below one-half of the median income—was also associated with higher crime rates. The former finding contradicts Fleisher (1966), but the latter finding on the role of income inequality supports Fleisher's findings that inequality is associated with higher crime rates. Both Fleisher (1966, 136) and Ehrlich (1973, 555) considered the effect of unemployment on crime rates, viewing the unemployment rate in a community as a complementary indicator of income opportunities available in the legal labor market. [3] In their empirical studies, however, both authors find that unemployment rates were less important determinants of crime rates than income levels and distribution.

Another important factor related to the effect of economic conditions on crime is the level of education of the population, which can determine the expected rewards from both legal and criminal activities. In addition, Usher (1993) has argued that education may also have a "civilization" effect, tending to reduce the incidence of criminal activity. However, after controlling for income inequality and median income, Ehrlich (1975a, 333) found a positive and significant relationship between the average number of school years completed by the adult population (over 25 years) and particularly property crimes committed across the U.S. in 1960. Four possible explanations of this puzzling empirical finding were provided by the author. First, it is possible that education may raise the marginal product of labor in the crime industry to a greater extent than for legitimate economic pursuits (Ehrlich 1975a, 319). Second, higher average levels of education may be associated with less under-reporting of crimes (Ehrlich 1975a, 333). Third, it is possible that education indicators act as a "surrogate for the average permanent income in the population, thus reflecting potential gains to be had from crime, especially property crimes" (Ehrlich 1975a, 333). Finally, combined with the observation that income inequality raises crime rates, it is possible to infer that certain crime rates are "directly related to inequalities in schooling and on-the-job training" (Ehrlich 1975a, 335).

Together with the relationship between economic conditions and crime, one of the main issues in the pioneering studies of Becker (1968) and Ehrlich (1973, 1975b, 1981) was the assessment of the effects of police presence, convictions, and the severity of punishments on the level of criminal activity. Individuals who are considering whether to commit crimes are assumed to evaluate both the risk of being caught and the associated punishment. The empirical evidence from the United States confirmed that both factors have a negative effect on crime rates—see Ehrlich (1973, 545, and 1996, 55).

Analysts often make a subtle distinction between the "deterrence" effects of policing and convictions and the "incapacitation" effects of locking-up (or killing, in the case of capital punishment) criminals who may have a tendency to rejoin the crime industry once they are released.

As stated by Ehrlich (1981, 311), "deterrence essentially aims at modifying the 'price of crime' for all offenders," while incapacitation—and for that matter, rehabilitation—acts through the removal of, "a subset of convicted offenders from the market for offenses either by relocating them in legitimate labor markets, or by excluding them from the social scene for prescribed periods of time." The author showed that, in theory, the effectiveness of rehabilitation and incapacitation, vis-à-vis the purely deterrent approach to crime control, depends on the rate of recidivism of offenders, and on their responsiveness to economic incentives—i.e., changes in the "price of crime."[4] For example, the relatively higher rates of recidivism observed for property crimes—in comparison to violent crimes (Leung 1995, 66)—may imply that incapacitation and/or rehabilitation are more appropriate means for controlling these types of crime than deterrence policies. However, if property offenders respond readily to economic incentives, the argument would be the opposite.

Since most forms of punishment that incapacitate offenders also involve deterrent effects—e.g. imprisonment—it is often difficult to evaluate empirically the importance of each type of action. Using estimates based on regression results for the U.S. states in 1960, Ehrlich (1981) concluded that, "in practice the overwhelming portion of the total preventive effect of imprisonment is attributable to its pure deterrent effect." Moreover, Ehrlich (1975b) found that capital punishment provisions across the U.S. tended to reduce crime rates primarily through their deterrent effect, rather than through their incapacitation effect. Levitt (1995) addressed these issues jointly with one of the most recurrent problems in the aforementioned literature; namely, the author attempts to assess whether the seemingly negative relationship between crime rates and arrest rates were the product of deterrence effects, incapacitation, or measurement errors associated with the fact that crime tends to go unreported.[5] The author finds that most of this negative relationship in the U.S. is due to deterrence effects, and not measurement error or incapacitation, for most types of crime.

Another important consideration for assessing the effectiveness of deterrence is the individual's attitude towards risk, because an individual's expected utility from illegal income will be affected by his/her tastes for the risk involved. Becker (1968, 178) and Ehrlich (1973, 528), for example, established that a risk-neutral offender will tend to spend more time in criminal activity than a risk-averse individual. Another implication of assuming risk-aversion is that raising the probability of conviction may have a greater deterrent effect than raising the severity of punishment (Becker 1968, 178).

Some recent contributions to the theoretical literature consider the possible endogeneity of the perceived probability of punishment of offenders, and emphasize that the timing of the rewards and punishments from crime will affect the incidence of criminal activity over time. Davis (1988), for example, considers a model where the probability of a criminal being caught at any point in time is positively related to both the intensity of the individual's criminal activity, and to the rate of enforcement at that point in time. The author stresses that this probability is a component of the rate used by potential offenders to discount future streams of income from illegal activities, and derives optimal crime rates for given levels of punishment and rates of enforcement. Leung (1995) extends this type of model by considering an infinite time horizon, and by introducing recidivism into the analysis. The author allows the individual's number of previous convictions to affect the probability of a new conviction when a past offender commits new crimes, as well as the severity of the corresponding punishment. In Leung's (1995) model, past criminal records also reduce the returns from engaging in legal activities, both through stigma and human capital effects. The latter are associated with the depreciation of past skills and the foregoing of new investments in education during the period spent on illegal activities or in jail.

Sah (1991) studied a different relationship between the intensity of crime rates over time and the probability of apprehension. The author argued that individuals living in areas with high crime-participation rates can perceive a lower probability of apprehension than those living in areas with low crime-participation rates, because the resources spent in apprehending each criminal tend to be low in high crime areas. An important implication of this analysis is that "past crime breeds future crime" (Sah 1991, 1282). In a similar analysis, Posada (1994) presented a simple model where a random increase in crime rates can result in a permanent increase in the crime rate, when the increase in crime is not compensated by a proportional increase in the resources spent in the detection and punishment of crimes, which results in a lower perceived rate of apprehension.

Glaeser, Sacerdote, and Scheinkman (1996) emphasized the role of local social interactions in determining crime rates in U.S. cities. In contrast to Sah (1991) and Posada (1994), who emphasized the effect of what we call "systemic" interactions (i.e., an individual's perceived probability of apprehension depends on society's crime rate), Glaeser et al. (1996) argued that "local" interactions among individuals act through the transfer of information between agents regarding, "criminal techniques and the returns to crime, or interactions result from the inputs of family members and peers that determine the costs of crime or the taste for crime (i.e., family values), and monitoring by close neighbors" (Glaeser, et al. 1996, 512). A notable implication of the local interactions approach is that crime rates across communities need not converge. For the purposes of this paper, the implication of systemic and local interactions is that countries may experience criminal inertia over time.

In sum, the economics literature on crime has transited from an emphasis on economic conditions (including education) and deterrence effects to more recent considerations of factors that may explain how crime is propagated over time and within communities. In the following section we attempt to organize some of the ideas addressed in the literature in a simple framework.

A SIMPLE, REDUCED-FORM MODEL OF CRIMINAL BEHAVIOR

WE NOW PRESENT A SIMPLE MODEL of criminal behavior that may help us organize ideas and motivate the variables postulated as determinants of crime rates in the empirical section of the paper.[6] We first model criminal behavior from the perspective of the individual and then aggregate to the national level to obtain a reduced-form equation of the causes of national crime rates.

The basic assumptions are that potential criminals act rationally, basing their decision to commit a crime on an analysis of the costs and benefits associated with a particular criminal act. Furthermore, we assume that individuals are risk neutral, and respond to changes in the probability of apprehension and the severity of punishment. Thus, individuals will commit a crime whenever its expected net benefits are large enough. Equation (1) below says that, for a particular individual, the expected net benefit (*nb*) of committing a crime is equal to its expected payoff (that is, the probability of not being apprehended *(1-pr)* times the loot *l*), minus the total costs associated with planning and executing the crime (*c*), minus the foregone wages from legitimate activities (*w*), minus the expected punishment for the committed crime (*pr*pu*):[7]

$$nb = (1\text{-}pr) \star l - c - w - pr \star pu \qquad \textbf{(1)}$$

Assuming that individuals have some "moral values," the expected net benefits of a crime would have to exceed a certain threshold before she/he commits a crime. The individual's threshold would be determined by her/his moral stance (*m*), to which we can assign a pecuniary value to make it comparable to the other variables in the model. Equation (2) establishes this relationship between the decision to commit a crime and the net benefits of such behavior:

$$\begin{aligned} d &= 1 \text{ when } nb \geq = m \\ d &= 0 \text{ when } nb < = m \end{aligned} \qquad \textbf{(2)}$$

where *d* stands for the decision to commit the crime ($d = 1$) or not to commit the crime ($d = 0$).

In the empirical section of the paper, we estimate a model in which the dependent variable is the national crime rate and the explanatory variables are a number of national economic and social characteristics. We first link those characteristics with the elements entering the individual decision to commit a crime. Then, we aggregate over individuals in a nation to obtain a reduced-form expression for the country's crime rate in terms of the underlying socio-economic variables. (Box 1 summarizes the discussion below.)

The first underlying variable is individual **education** (*e*), which may impact on the decision to commit a crime through several channels. Higher levels of educational attainment may be associated with higher expected legal earnings, thus raising *w*. Also, education, through its civic component, may increase the individual's moral stance, *m*. On the other hand, education may reduce the costs of committing crimes (i.e., reducing *c*) or may raise the crime's loot, *l*, because education may open opportunities for an individual to enter higher-paying crime industries. Hence the net effect of education on the individual's decision to commit a crime is, *a priori*, ambiguous. We can conjecture, however, that if legal economic activities are more skill- or education-intensive than illegal activities, then it is more likely that education will induce individuals not to commit crimes. In addition, following Tauchen and Witte (1994), it is possible that school enrollment alone (independently of the level of educational attainment) will reduce the time available for participating in the crime industry. Hence, the empirical section will assess the effect of both secondary enrollment rates and educational attainment on crime rates.

The **individual's past experience in criminal activities** (d_{t-1}) is another important underlying variable that affects in several ways the decision to commit a crime. First, convicts tend to be stigmatized in the legal labor market, thus having diminished employment opportunities and expected income (lower *w*). Second, criminals can learn by doing, which means that the costs of carrying out criminal acts, *c*, may decline over time. Third, people tend to have a reduced moral threshold, *m*, after having joined the crime industry. The **past incidence of crime in society** (D_{t-1}), through the local social interactions noted in our literature survey, also affect the individual's decision by both reducing the costs of carrying out criminal activities (lower *c*) and impairing civic moral values (lower *m*). These arguments strongly suggest the possibility of criminal inertia, that is, present crime incidence explained to some extent by its past incidence.

The **level and growth of economic activity** (*EA*) in society create attractive opportunities for employment in the legal sector (higher *w*) but, since they also improve the wealth of other members of society, the size of the potential loot from crime, *l*, also rises. Therefore, the effect of heightened economic activity on the individual's decision to commit a crime is, in principle, ambiguous. The effect of **income inequality** in society (*INEQ*) will depend on the individual's relative income position. It is likely that in the case of the rich, an increase in inequality will not induce them to commit more crimes. However, in the case of the poor, an increase in inequality may be crime inducing, because such an increase implies a larger gap between the poor's wages and those of the rich, thus reflecting a larger difference between the income from criminal and legal activities (higher *l-w*). A rise in inequality may also have a crime-inducing effect by reducing the individual's moral threshold (lower *m*) through what we could call an "envy effect." Therefore, a rise inequality will have a positive impact on (at least some) individuals' propensity to commit a crime.

The **existence of profitable criminal activities** (*DRUGS*) in some countries means that the expected loot from crime is larger in those countries than in others. The most important example of profitable criminal activities is the illicit drug trade (other two are gambling and prostitution). Countries where the raw materials for illicit drugs are easily obtained (such as Colombia, Bolivia, and Peru in the case of cocaine) or countries that are located close to high drug consumption centers (such as Mexico in relation to the United States) have frequent and highly profitable opportunities for criminal activities. These activities not only consist of drug production and trade themselves, but also involve the element of violence and official corruption required for them to carry on.

The **strength of the police and the judicial system** (*JUST*) increases the probability of apprehension (*pr*) and the punishment (*pu*) for criminal actions, thus reducing the incentive for an individual to commit a crime. This is the crime deterrence effect. It should also be noted that the past incidence of crime in society (D_{t-1}) may determine an individual's perceived probability of apprehension (*pr*) via systemic interactions, as discussed above.

Finally, there are **other factors** that may affect an individual's propensity to commit crimes (*other*) such as cultural characteristics (religion and colonial heritage, for example), age and sex (young males are said to be more violent prone than the rest of the population), the availability of fire arms in the country, and the population density where the individual lives (urban centers would facilitate the social interaction through which crime skills are transmitted). These other factors can affect the individual's decision to commit a crime mainly through the cost of planning and executing the crime (*c*) and through his/her moral threshold (*m*).

Considering the effects summarized in Box 1, and substituting them into equations (1) and (2), we have that a given individual will commit a crime if the following inequality holds,

$$d=1 \text{ if}$$

$$I(\overset{+}{e}, \overset{+}{EA}, \overset{+}{INEQ}, \overset{+}{DRUGS}, \overset{-}{JUST}) - c(\overset{-}{e}, \overset{-}{d_{t-1}}, \overset{-}{D_{t-1}}, \overset{-}{other}) \tag{3}$$

$$- w(\overset{+}{e}, \overset{-}{d_{t-1}}, \overset{+}{EA}) - pr(\overset{+}{JUST}) * pu - m(\overset{+}{e}, \overset{-}{d_{t-1}}, \overset{-}{D_{t-1}}, \overset{-}{INEQ}, \overset{-}{other}) \geq 0$$

Rewriting this condition as a function *f* of the underlying individual and social variables, we obtain the following reduced-form expression,

$$d=1 \text{ if}$$

$$f(\overset{?}{e}, \overset{+}{d_{t-1}}, \overset{+}{D_{t-1}}, \overset{?}{EA}, \overset{+}{INEQ}, \overset{+}{DRUGS}, \overset{-}{JUST}, \overset{+}{other}) \geq 0 \tag{4}$$

$$f(\Psi_t) \geq 0$$

where Ψ is a vector of the underlying determinants of crime. Assuming *both* a linear probability model for the decision to commit a crime and a linear functional form for *f*, we obtain the following individual regression equation,

$$d = \beta'\Psi + \mu \tag{5}$$

The assumption of linearity in both the functional form of *f* and the probability model are, of course, arbitrary. They are chosen because they allow the aggregation of equation (5). Given that our data is not individual but national, our regression equation must be specified in terms of national rates, which is obtained by averaging equation (5) over all individuals in a country and over a given time period,

$$D_t = \beta'\Psi_t + v_t \tag{6}$$

That is,

$$\begin{aligned} \textit{Crime rate}_{i,t} = {} & \beta_0 + \beta_1 \, EDUC_{i,t} + \beta_2 \, \textit{Lagged crime rate}_{i,t} + \beta_3 \, EA_{i,t} \\ & + \beta_4 \, DRUGS_{i,t} + \beta_5 \, JUST_{i,t} + \beta_6 \, OTHER_{i,t} + \eta_i + \epsilon_{i,t} \end{aligned} \tag{7}$$

where the subscripts *I* and *t* represent country and time period, respectively; and η is an unobserved country-specific effect.

Box 1.

Underlying Determinants of Criminal Activities

Individual education (*e*): $\uparrow e \Rightarrow \uparrow I, \downarrow c, \uparrow w, \uparrow m$

Individual criminal experience (d_{t-1}): $\uparrow d_{t-1} \Rightarrow \downarrow c, \downarrow w, \downarrow m$

Past incidence of crime in society (D_{t-1}): $\uparrow D_{t-1} \Rightarrow \downarrow c, \downarrow m$

Level and growth of economic activity (*EA*): $\uparrow EA \Rightarrow \uparrow I, \uparrow w$

Income inequality (*INEQ*): $\uparrow INEQ \Rightarrow \uparrow (I-w), \downarrow m$

Existence of profitable criminal activities (*DRUGS*): $\uparrow DRUGS \Rightarrow \uparrow I$

Strength of police and justice system (*JUST*): $\uparrow JUST \Rightarrow \uparrow pr, \uparrow pu$

Other factors that affect the propensity to commit a crime (*other*): $\uparrow other \Rightarrow \downarrow c, \downarrow m$

IV THE DATA

A FULL DESCRIPTION OF THE VARIABLES (and their sources) used in this paper is presented in the Appendix. Curious readers are urged to examine the descriptions and tables included therein. This section briefly describes the data used to calculate the national crime rates and the set of explanatory variables.

A. National Crime Rates

The empirical implementation of the theoretical model proposed above will rely on crime rates, which were based on the number of crimes reported by national justice ministries to the United Nations World Crime Surveys. The econometric analysis will focus on the determinants of "intentional homicide," and robbery rates between 1970 and 1994.[8] All crime rates are expressed as the number of reported crimes in each category per 100,000 inhabitants. As shown in Table 1, there is a considerable variation in the crime variables. However, it is worth noting that most countries did not report data for the entire period nor for every type of crime.

A major issue associated with official reported crime statistics is that they suffer from under-reporting. We deal with this problem in three ways. First, we focus on intentional homicide rates, which tend to suffer less under-reporting than other crime data. The analysis uses robbery rates only for comparative purposes, and some econometric tests to be discussed below reveal that many of the model specifications applied to robbery rates were incorrect, and hence the results are irrelevant. Second, as explained in the Appendix, we carefully clean the time series data for each country by eliminating observations that show suspicious changes in the magnitude of the reported number of intentional homicides and robberies. Third, the panel data techniques used in the econometric exercises effectively eliminate some of the statistical inference problems that may arise from a probable correlation between some of the explanatory variable (such as the level of education of the population and the conviction rate) and the extent of under-reporting of crime rates.

Figure 1 shows the evolution of the population-weighted average rate of intentional homicides in the group of 34 countries for which there was data available in each five-year subperiod. As mentioned in the introduction, the world's intentional homicide rate has been increasing steadily, at least since the early 1980s,

Table 1. Summary Statistics for Crime

Variables	*No. of Obs.*	*Mean*	*Standard Deviation*	*Min.*	*Max.*	*No. of Countries*
Crime Rates:*						
Intentional Homicides	1579	6.834	11.251	0	142.014	128
Robbery	1251	55.902	95.973	0	676.840	120

* Per 100,000 inhabitants, annual data.

with a notable acceleration during recent years. Figures 2 and 3 show the evolution of the median intentional homicide rate in each five-year period for the whole sample of countries, while separating groups of countries by income levels and regions. We use the median rate to describe the evolution of homicide rates because this measure is less sensitive to the influence of outliers than the mean rate. Figure 2 shows that much of the increase was due to increases in the median homicide rates of middle-low and low-income countries (where the former had a GNP per capita ranging from $766 [US dollars] in 1995 to $3,035, and the latter had an income per capita of $765 or less). Figure 3 shows that the highest homicide rates are found in Latin America and the Caribbean, followed by Sub-Saharan Africa. In these regions, and in the developing countries of Europe and Central Asia, considerable increases in intentional homicide rates have been observed in the early 1990s. However, it should be noted that the sample of Sub-Saharan African countries is quite small and varies across sub-periods, thus the evolution of the median rate for this group may reflect the inclusion of outliers in the latter two periods (e.g., Swaziland and São Tomé & Principe have high crime rates, but we only have data for the last two periods).

Figures 4 and 5 show the evolution of intentional homicide rates in South America and Mexico, and in Central America, the Caribbean, Guyana, and Suriname respectively.[9] Regarding Figure 4, it is interesting to note that only Argentina and Chile experienced a decline in their homicide rates since the early 1970s, when both countries faced severe economic and political crises. Colombia experienced the most noticeable increase in the homicide rate, jumping from an average of approximately 16 intentional homicides per 100,000 inhabitants during 1970–74 to over 80 in 1990–94, possibly reflecting the rise of the drug trafficking industry in that country. Figure 5 shows that several small economies, such as Bahamas, Jamaica, Nicaragua, and El Salvador, have had higher intentional homicide rates than most large Latin American countries. All of these countries have experienced rates in excess of 20 intentional homicides per 100,000 population. Furthermore, Bahamas, Barbados, Jamaica, and Trinidad and Tobago have experienced considerable increases in their crime

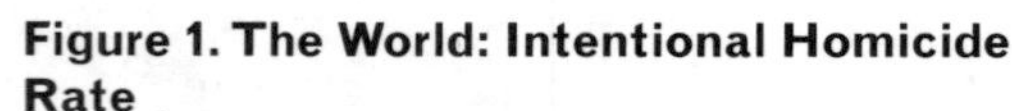
Figure 1. The World: Intentional Homicide Rate
(population-weighted average)

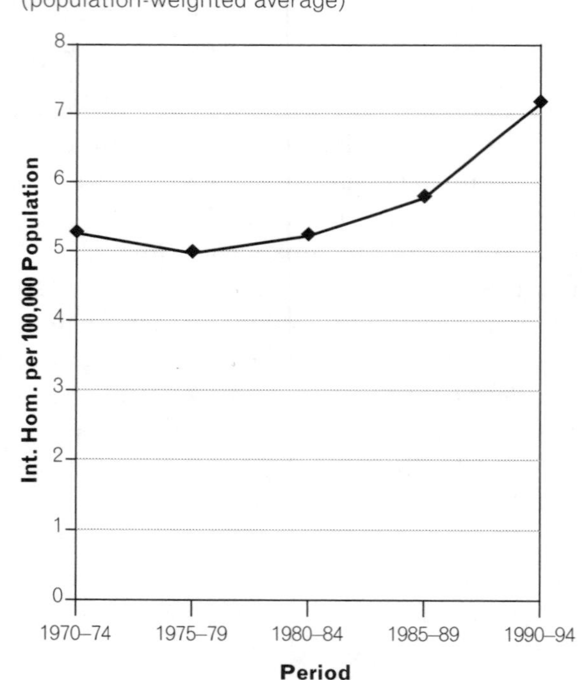

Note: Weighted average calculated using the following sample of 34 countries: Argentina, Australia, Austria, The Bahamas, Bahrain, Barbados, Bulgaria, Canada, Colombia, Costa Rica, Cyprus, Denmark, Arab Republic of Egypt, Germany, Greece, India, Indonesia, Italy, Japan, the Republic of Korea, Kuwait, Malaysia, Mexico, Norway, Poland, Qatar, Singapore, Spain, Sweden, Syrian Arab Republic, Thailand, Trinidad and Tobago, United States, and Venezuela.

Figure 2. Median Intentional Homicide Rates by Income Groups, 1970–94

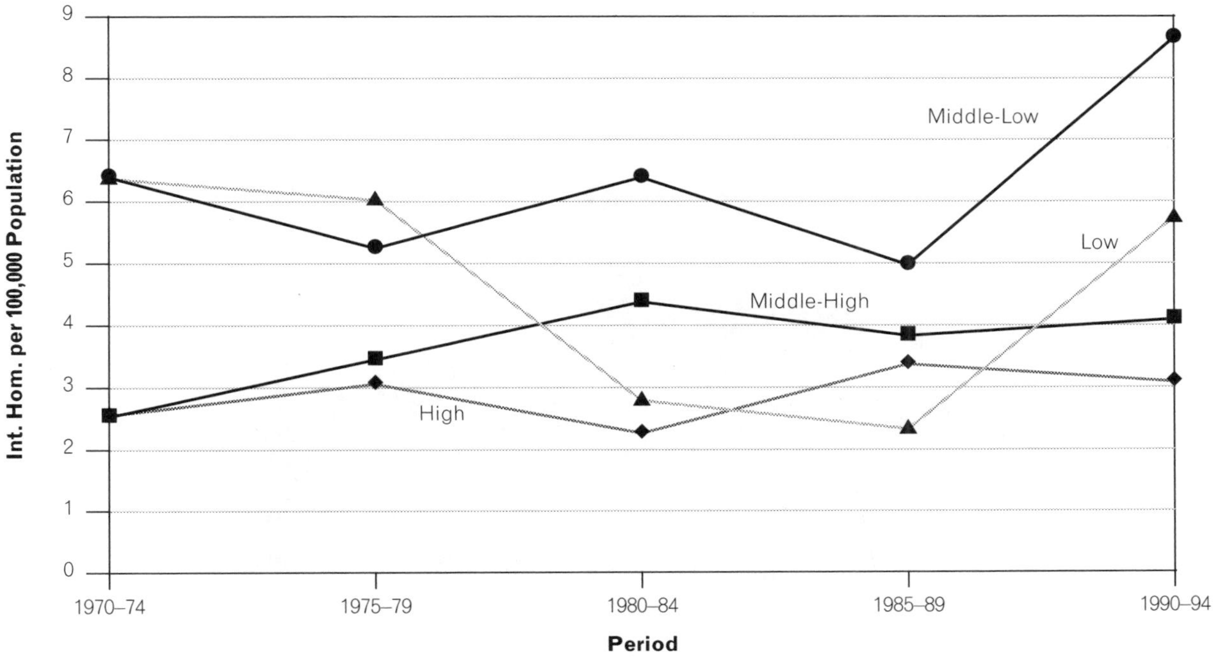

9
8
7
6
5
4
3
2
1
0
Int. Hom. per 100,000 Population
Middle-Low
Low
Middle-High
High
1970–74
1975–79
1980–84
1985–89
1990–94
Period

Notes: Income groups are defined in terms of annual per capita income. Low income = $765 or less; middle-low = $766–$4,035; middle-high = $3,036–$9,386; high = more than $9,386, based on GNP per capita as of 1995.

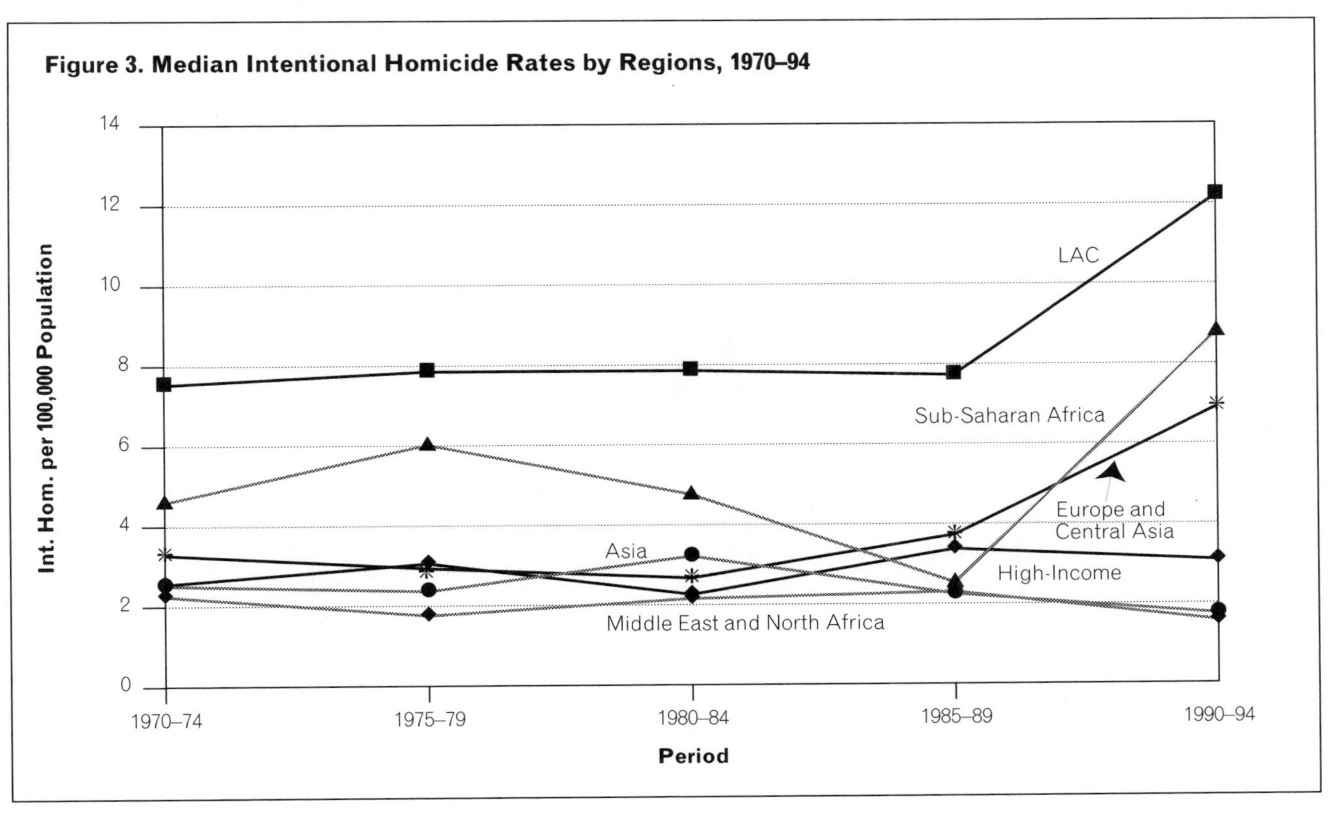

Figure 3. Median Intentional Homicide Rates by Regions, 1970–94

14
12
10
8
6
4
2
0
Int. Hom. per 100,000 Population
LAC
Sub-Saharan Africa
Europe and
Central Asia
Asia
High-Income
Middle East and North Africa
1970–74
1975–79
1980–84
1985–89
1990–94
Period

Figure 4. Intentional Homicide Rates in South America and Mexico, 1970–94

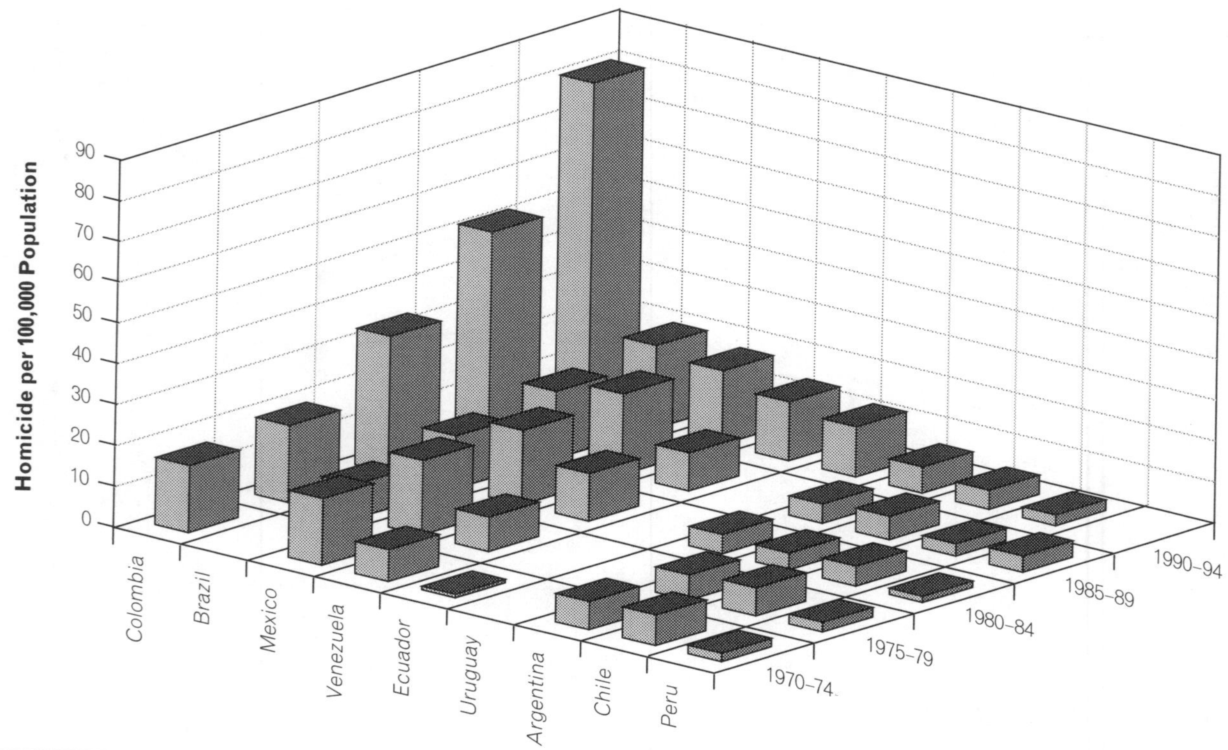

Figure 5. Intentional Homicide Rates in Central America, the Caribbean, Guyana, and Suriname, 1970–94

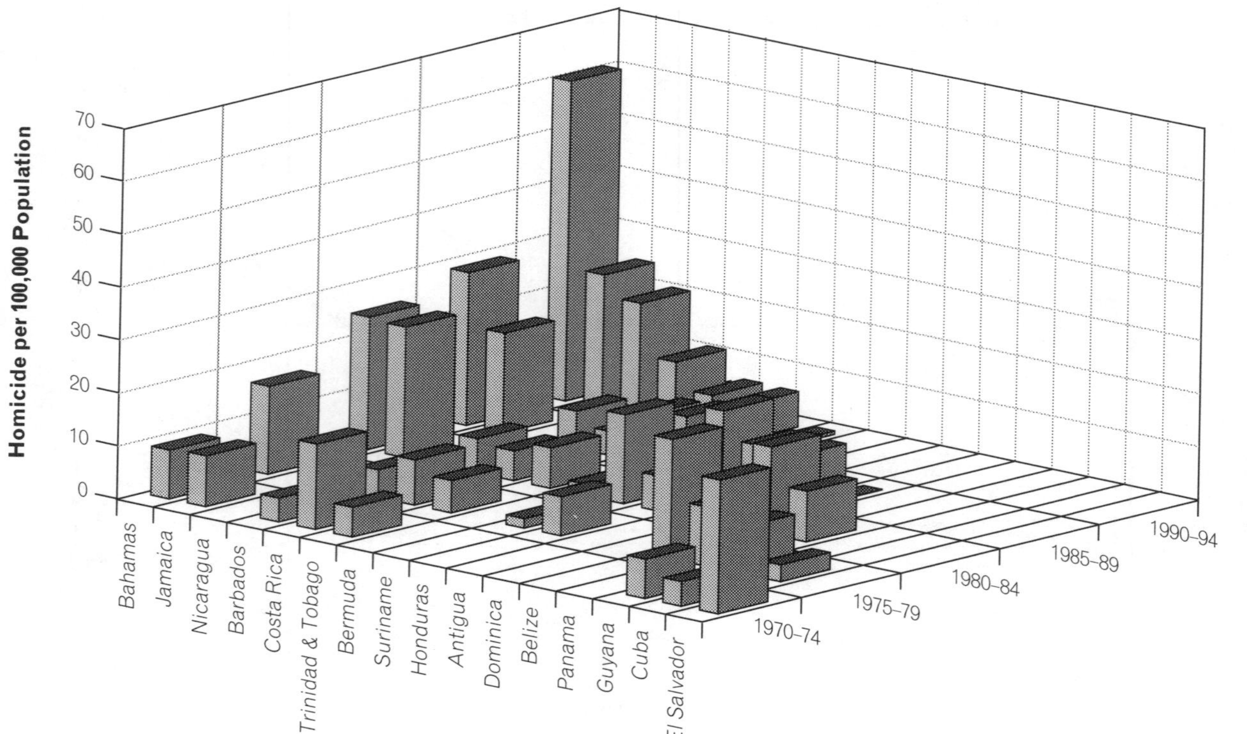

rates since the early 1970s. Of the small countries, only Costa Rica has experienced a steady decline of its intentional homicide rate. Thus, the rise in the overall homicide rate in Latin America and the Caribbean can be attributed to an upward trend in criminal activity in most countries of the region (with a few exceptions such as Argentina, Chile, and Costa Rica), with a few outliers that have experienced dramatic increases in criminal activity (Bahamas, Jamaica, and Colombia).

B. Explanatory Variables

Following the simple model presented in the previous section, we have selected a set of explanatory variables that proxy for the main economic determinants of crime rates, as well as for some of the non-pecuniary factors that may affect the decision to perform illegal activities.

As a proxy of the average income of the countries involved in our econometric study, we use the (log of) Gross National Product (GNP) per capita, in prices of 1987. The figures were converted to U.S. dollars on the basis of the methodology proposed by Loayza et al. (1998), which is based on an average of real exchange rates.[10] In the regressions that are based on both cross-sectional and time-series data, we also used the rate of growth of GDP, calculated on the basis of figures expressed in 1987 prices (in local currency).

The degree of income inequality was measured by the Gini index and by the percentage of the national income received by the lowest quintile of a country's income. Both variables were constructed on the basis of the data set provided by Deininger and Squire (1996); we used what these authors have termed "high quality" data for the countries and years for which it was available, and otherwise calculated an average of alternative figures (also provided by Deininger and Squire, 1996). The Gini coefficients which were originally based on expenditure information were adjusted to ensure their comparability with the coefficients based on income data.[11]

Two educational variables were used, as measures of the stock and the flow of investment in human capital in a given country. These are, respectively, the average years of schooling of the population over 15 years of age, as calculated by Barro and Lee (1996), and the secondary enrollment rate, which was taken from World Bank databases, and is defined as the number of people (of all ages) enrolled in secondary schools, expressed as a percentage of the total population of secondary school age.[12]

Another type of economic incentive to commit crime that we considered was the existence of profitable criminal "industries." In particular, we focused on the existence, in a given country, of considerable production and/or distribution of illegal drugs. The choice of this particular crime industry was motivated not only by the fact that the drug trade is known to be highly profitable but also because, at least in some countries—e.g. the U.S.—it is also known to use a very "violence-intensive" technology. The latter aspect of this industry, and the intellectual and moral decay associated with the consumption of the substances in question, can be expected to generate externalities for the proliferation of other violent crimes. We used two specific variables as measures of the size of the illegal drug industry. The first was the number of drug possession offenses per 100,000 population, which we calculated on the basis of data from the United Nations' World Crime Surveys. It is worth noting that this variable does not measure the extent of actual drug consumption in a given country, but only the fraction of that figure that is considered illegal in the country's legislation, and that has been detected by the law enforcement agencies. Thus, the variable in question reflects not only the size of the drug-consuming population, but also the degree of tolerance for drug consumption in the corresponding society. The second measure that we used is a "dummy" variable that takes the value one when a country is listed as a significant producer of any illegal drug in any of the issues of the U.S. Department of State's *International Narcotics Control Strategy Report*—which has been published on an annual basis since 1986.

Regarding the negative incentives to commit crime, we used several variables to proxy for the probability of being caught and convicted when performing an illegal activity, and for the corresponding severity of the punishments. To capture the first component of the crime deterrence efforts of a given society, we used both the number of police personnel per 100,000 inhabitants, and the conviction rate of the corresponding crime, defined as the ratio of the number of convictions to the number of reported occurrences of each type of crime, both of which were constructed on the basis of data provided by the United Nations in its World Crime Surveys. We also collected information provided by Amnesty International about the existence of the death penalty in countries across the globe, which we use as an indicator of the severity of punishments.

Other determinants of the intensity of criminal activity highlighted by the theoretical model presented above include factors that reduce both the pecuniary and the non-pecuniary cost of engaging in illegal activities. These factors may act by facilitating the development of social interactions between criminals and would-be criminals. Assuming that these interactions are more prevalent in urban agglomerations than in rural areas, we use the rate of urbanization as a possible factor in explaining crime rates across nations. We also include in our empirical exercise the proportion of the total population encompassed by males belonging to the 15–29 age group, which is—at least in the U.S.—the demographic group to which most criminals belong.

The taste or preference for criminal activity may also be influenced by cultural characteristics of the countries involved. As countries with common cultural traits may also share similar economic characteristics, it is important to control for the former in order to obtain an accurate appraisal of the effect of the latter on the determination of national crime rates. With this end in mind, we employed religion and regional "dummies" in our cross-sectional regressions. The first set of variables—related to Buddhist, Christian, Hindu, and Muslim countries—was constructed on the basis of information from the *CIA Factbook*, and each variable takes the value one for the countries in which the corresponding religion is the one with the largest number of followers. Regional dummies were constructed for the developing countries of Sub-Saharan Africa, Asia, Europe and Central Asia, Latin America and the Caribbean, Middle East and Northern Africa, all based on the regional definitions employed by the World Bank and the International Monetary Fund. Finally, we used a variable from Easterly and Levine (1997) that measures the likelihood that two randomly selected people from a given country will not belong to the same ethno-linguistic group. This index is only available for 1960, and hence it should be interpreted with caution. The objective is to capture not only cultural effects on crime that may be derived from a common set of values, but also any potential effects from cultural polarization.

EMPIRICAL IMPLEMENTATION

A VERSION OF THE REGRESSION EQUATION derived from our model is first run for simple cross-sections and then applied to panel data. On the one hand, cross-sectional regressions are illustrative because they emphasize cross-country variation of the data, allowing us to analyze the effects of variables that do not change much over time. On the other hand, working with panel data (that is, pooled cross-country and time-series data) allows us to consider both the effect of the business cycle (i.e., GDP growth rate) on the crime rate and the presence of criminal inertia (accounted for by the inclusion of lagged crime rate as an explanatory variable). Furthermore, the use of panel data will allow us to account for unobserved country-specific effects, for the likely joint endogeneity of some of the explanatory variables, and for some types of measurement errors in the reported crime rates.

As dependent variables, we consider the incidence of two types of crime, namely, intentional homicide and robbery. Under-reporting is a major problem related to the available measures of crime. It is well known that mis-measurement of the dependent variable does not lead to estimation biases when the measurement error is uncorrelated with the regressors. This condition, however, is very likely to be violated in the case of crime under-reporting given that the degree of mis-measurement is surely related, for instance, to the average income of the population, its level of education, and the degree of income inequality, which are considered as explanatory variables in our empirical model of crime. Of all types of crime, intentional homicide is the one that suffers the least from under-reporting because corpses are more difficult to ignore than losses of property or assaults. Therefore, most of the analysis will concentrate on the regressions that have the intentional homicide rate as the dependent variable. To the extent that intentional homicide is a good proxy for overall crime, the conclusions we reach apply also to criminal behavior broadly understood. However, if intentional homicide proxies mostly for violent crime, then our results apply more narrowly. Hence we also focus on the determinants of robbery rates. Robberies are crimes against property that include a violent component; they are defined as the taking away of property from a person, overcoming resistance by force or threat of force. We believe that victims of robberies may have stronger incentives to report them than victims of only theft or assault.

For ease of exposition, we first present the cross-sectional regression results and then the panel regression results.

A. Cross-Sectional Regressions

Tables 2 and 3 report the results from cross-sectional regressions (for the log) of intentional homicides and robbery rates, respectively. These regressions use country averages of the relevant dependent variables for the period 1970–94, but the averages were calculated using only the

Table 2. OLS Cross-Sectional Regressions of the Log of Intentional Homicide Rates
(p-values in parenthesis)

	(1)	(2)	(3)	(4)	(5)	(6)	(7)
Log of GNP per Capita	-.004 (.981)	-.096 (.577)	-.278 (.125)	-.090 (.649)	.014 (.935)	-.078 (.628)	-.032 (.885)
Gini Index	.035 (.019)		.035 (.034)	.038 (.025)	.043 (.014)	.052 (.002)	.041 (.025)
Average Years of Schooling	-.027 (.744)	-.017 (.814)		.011 (.901)	.013 (.885)	.079 (.384)	-.052 (.598)
Urbanization Rate	.000 (.989)	.002 (.791)	.004 (.625)	.005 (.593)	.001 (.920)	.001 (.919)	-.001 (.886)
Drug Producers Dummy	.670 (.074)	.912 (.012)	.390 (.272)	.711 (.069)	1.305 (.002)	1.311 (.001)	.667 (.093)
Drug Possession Crimes Rate	.002 (.329)	.001 (.694)	.003 (.090)	.002 (.359)	.001 (.616)	.001 (.758)	.004 (.127)
Income Share of the Poorest Quintile		-20.405 (.001)					
Secondary Enrollment Rate			.009 (.314)				
Police				-.001 (.214)			
Conviction Rate					-.001 (.001)	-.002 (.000)	
Death Penalty						-.659 (.011)	
Index of Ethno-Linguistic Fractionalization							-.665 (.200)
Constant	-.066 (.963)	3.190 (.003)	1.109 (.396)	.213 (.885)	-.755 (.619)	-.322 (.821)	.270 (.887)
R^2	.285	.386	.213	.303	.502	.599	.311
Adjusted R^2	.200	.306	.127	.192	.405	.501	.198
Number of Observations	58	53	62	52	44	42	51

annual observations for which the homicide data was available.

Table 2 shows that the Gini index of income distribution has a positive coefficient, which is significant in all the regressions, revealing that countries with more unequal distributions of income tend to have higher crime rates than those with more egalitarian patterns of income distribution. In addition, regression (2) includes an alternative measure of the distribution of income; namely, the share of national income received by the poorest 20 percent of the population. The negative and significant coefficient of this variable tells us that crime tends to decline as the poorest quintile receives higher shares of national income. Income (i.e., log of GNP) per capita seems to be negatively associated with the incidence of intentional homicides, as reflected in its negative coefficient, but this result is significant at conventional levels in only one of the sixteen regressions presented in Table 2. The combination of an insignificant effect of the income per capita with a significant effect of the distribution of income may indicate that changes in income distribution, rather than changes in the absolute

Table 2. Continued

	(8)	(9)	(10)	(11)	(12)	(13)	(14)	(15)	(16)
Log of GNP per Capita	-.006 (.974)	-.077 (.674)	-.038 (.831)	-.069 (.708)	-.030 (.870)	-.132 (.489)	.012 (.948)	.046 (.801)	-.024 (.898)
Gini Index	.035 (.021)	.031 (.041)	.030 (.048)	.028 (.073)	.029 (.076)	.029 (.059)	.038 (.015)	.024 (.143)	.034 (.027)
Average Years of Schooling	-.028 (.735)	-.060 (.474)	-.049 (.559)	-.073 (.409)	-.025 (.768)	-.009 (.911)	-.046 (.595)	-.042 (.611)	-.038 (.660)
Urbanization Rate	.000 (.977)	.001 (.931)	-.001 (.944)	.002 (.813)	.002 (.808)	-.004 (.666)	.001 (.915)	-.004 (.612)	.001 (.882)
Drug Producers Dummy	.653 (.087)	.624 (.090)	.706 (.057)	.582v (.121)	.760 (.049)	.751 (.043)	.690 (.067)	.558 (.135)	.633 (.097)
Drug Possession Crimes Rate	.002 (.328)	.003 (.196)	.002 (.232)	.003 (.214)	.002 (.359)	.002 (.273)	.002 (.247)	.002 (.255)	.002 (.312)
Buddhist Dummy (most common religion)	.140 (.737)								
Christian Dummy (most common religion)		.437 (.087)							
Hindu Dummy (most common religion)			-.816 (.111)						
Muslim Dummy (most common religion)				-.541 (.158)					
Sub-Saharan Africa Dummy					.457 (.307)				
South and East Asia Dummy						-.663 (.073)			
Eastern Europe and Central Asia Dummy							.321 (.412)		
Latin America Dummy								.488 (.110)	
Middle East Dummy									-.378 (.530)
Constant	-.052 (.971)	.545 (.702)	.605 (.675)	.967 (.538)	.232 (.872)	1.420 (.376)	-.275 (.848)	.226 (.871)	.159 (.913)
R^2	.286	.326	.320	.313	.299	.330	.294	.320	.290
Adjusted R^2	.186	.231	.225	.217	.201	.236	.195	.225	.191
Number of Observations	58	58	58	58	58	58	58	58	58

levels of poverty, are associated with changes in violent crime rates.

Regarding education, the results in Table 2 show that the average years of schooling, or the level of educational attainment of the population, has a negative coefficient in 12 out of the 15 regressions that include this variable, but the coefficient is not significant in any specification. In equation (3) we use the secondary enrollment rate (or the flow of human capital) instead of the attainment variable. Contrary to our expectations, the coefficient of the enrollment rate is positive, but also insignificant. As elaborated in our theoretical model, the relationship between educational variables and crime rates can be ambiguous. However, from an empirical point of view, these results may be explained by an implicit relationship between the extent of crime under-reporting and the level of education of the population; that is, an increase in education may induce people to report more crimes, thus producing a rise in *reported* crime rates. Also, the two education variables are in fact negatively correlated with the homicide rate and at the same time highly correlated with

Table 3. OLS Cross-Sectional Regressions of the Log of Intentional Robbery Rates
(p-values in parenthesis)

	(1)	*(2)*	*(3)*	*(4)*	*(5)*	*(6)*	*(7)*
Log of GNP per Capita	.061	-.169	-.127	-.129	-.101	-.161	.280
	(.821)	(.556)	(.616)	(.653)	(.741)	(.619)	(.430)
Gini Index	.091		.089	.085	.052	.060	.108
	(.000)		(.000)	(.001)	(.098)	(.082)	(.000)
Average Years of Schooling	.113	-.021		.133	-.033	-.028	.061
	(.360)	(.861)		(.290)	(.825)	(.856)	(.673)
Urbanization Rate	.020	.030	.022	.023	.025	.025	.020
	(.108)	(.023)	(.040)	(.070)	(.062)	(.078)	(.121)
Drug Producers Dummy	.139	.378	.206	.154	.699	.673	.276
	(.795)	(.517)	(.682)	(.774)	(.336)	(.370)	(.637)
Drug Possession Crimes Rate	.004	.005	.004	.004	.005	.005	.004
	(.223)	(.155)	(.097)	(.131)	(.111)	(.115)	(.229)
Income Share of the Poorest Quintile		-27.715					
		(.006)					
Secondary Enrollment Rate			.021				
			(.111)				
Police				.002			
				(.132)			
Conviction Rate					-.003	-.001	
					(.697)	(.885)	
Death Penalty						-.567	
						(.289)	
Index of Ethno-Linguistic Fractionalization							.349
							(.663)
Constant	-2.851	4.447	-2.055	-2.023	.694	1.146	-5.229
	(.179)	(.012)	(.246)	(.346)	(.807)	(.699)	(.100)
R^2	.452	.374	.469	.495	.404	.410	.460
Adjusted R^2	.375	.283	.402	.406	.264	.235	.355
Number of Observations	50	48	54	48	38	36	44

both per capita GNP (correlation about 0.5) and the Gini index (correlation about -0.55). Therefore, it is quite possible that the expected crime-reducing effects of education are captured by the measures of both national income per capita and income distribution, also present in the homicide rate regression equation. We will reconsider the effect of the educational variables when we discuss the panel data results.

Regressions (4)–(6) in Table 2 examine the relationship between deterrence and incapacitation effects and intentional homicide rates. The presence of police seems to reduce crime, but the negative coefficient is not significant. The coefficients corresponding to the conviction rate are statistically different from zero, even after including the variable that controls for the existence of the death penalty, which may indicate that high convictions rates tend to deter criminal activity independently of the incapacitation effect of the death penalty. However, as for most results of these OLS cross-sectional regressions, this result must be regarded as preliminary given that the negative relationship between homicide and con-

Table 3. Continued

	(8)	(9)	(10)	(11)	(12)	(13)	(14)	(15)	(16)
Log of GNP per Capita	.065 (.809)	-.061 (.812)	.073 (.790)	-.075 (.774)	.007 (.979)	-.213 (.465)	.026 (.922)	.135 (.596)	.061 (.821)
Gini Index	.092 (.000)	.088 (.000)	.093 (.000)	.076 (.001)	.072 (.006)	.077 (.001)	.088 (.000)	.067 (.005)	.091 (.000)
Average Years of Schooling	.114 (.354)	.018 (.881)	.121 (.340)	.009 (.942)	.125 (.302)	.130 (.274)	.142 (.259)	.082 (.480)	.113 (.360)
Urbanization Rate	.019 (.111)	.021 (.063)	.020 (.110)	.023 (.050)	.023 (.057)	.016 (.181)	.019 (.115)	.012 (.322)	.020 (.108)
Drug Producers Dummy	.201 (.708)	-.020 (.968)	.135 (.803)	-.044 (.932)	.429 (.439)	.177 (.731)	.087 (.870)	-.295 (.575)	.139 (.795)
Drug Possession Crimes Rate	.003 (.231)	.005 (.089)	.003 (.251)	.005 (.090)	.003 (.232)	.004 (.147)	.003 (.395)	.004 (.153)	.004 (.223)
Buddhist Dummy (most common religion)	-.639 (.271)								
Christian Dummy (most common religion)		1.054 (.007)							
Hindu Dummy (most common religion)			.249 (.735)						
Muslim Dummy (most common religion)				-1.420 (.019)					
Sub-Saharan Africa Dummy					1.083 (.105)				
South and East Asia Dummy						-1.127 (.042)			
Eastern Europe and Central Asia Dummy							-.648 (.268)		
Latin America Dummy								1.292 (.010)	
Middle East Dummy									dropped
Constant	-2.852 (.178)	-1.993 (.315)	-3.083 (.172)	-.569 (.796)	-2.069 (.330)	.222 (.929)	-2.467 (.249)	-2.007 (.315)	-2.851 (.179)
R^2	.468	.540	.453	.520	.485	.504	.468	.533	.452
Adjusted R^2	.379	.463	.362	.440	.400	.421	.379	.455	.375
Number of Observations	50	50	50	50	50	50	50	50	50

viction rates may be due to measurement error in the number of homicides, which is both the numerator of the homicide rate and the denominator of the conviction rate (see Levitt 1995).[13] We reexamine this issue in the context of panel data analysis, in which correction for measurement error is possible to some extent. In regressions not reported in Table 2, we included subjective indices of the quality of the state apparatus instead of the police and conviction rates. Neither the index of rule of law nor the index of absence of corruption turned out to be significant. The lack of significance of the estimated coefficients on these subjective indices of the rule of law and absence of corruption in the bureaucracy may be due to the fact that they are highly correlated with other important explanatory variables in the regression, namely, per capita GNP, the Gini index, and the measures of educational stand.

Table 2 also shows that the incidence of intentional homicides is statistically larger in countries that produce drugs. The drug possession crime rate, which proxies for the effects of both illegal drug consumption and for the violence emanating from the distribution of illegal drugs, is also positively associated with the intentional homicide rate, but it is significant in only two of the 16 specifications. These results give credence to the popular view that violent crimes increase with drug trafficking and consumption. It remains to be studied, however, whether the incidence of homicides in drug producing and/or consuming countries is directly affected by drug-related activities or is also the result of crime externalities of these activities. The latter would be the case if, for example, criminal organizations established to deal with drugs are also used to manage other forms of criminal endeavors.

In the cross-sectional regressions considered in Table 2, the urbanization rate appears not to be significantly associated with the homicide rate. This result may be due to the high correlation between the urbanization rate and other economic variables, such as income per capita, the Gini index, and, especially, the education variables. Still, we expected that the urbanization rate could provide information on the strength of social interactions in the formation of criminal behavior; this information would not be necessarily captured by the other indicators of economic development. We will reconsider this issue when discussing the robbery regressions and the panel data regressions for the homicide rate.

We examine the importance of other variables that in principle may be related to the incidence of intentional homicides. We do it by including them one by one in a core regression that considers per capita GNP, the Gini index, the average years of schooling, the urbanization rate, the drug producers dummy, and the drug possession crime rate as explanatory variables.[14] In these additional regressions (also presented in Table 2), we find the rather surprising result that the index of ethno-linguistic fractionalization, which has been used as a proxy for social polarization and conflict (see Easterly and Levine 1997), is negatively associated with the rate of intentional homicides, though this association is only marginally significant. Regarding the religion dummies, Christian countries seem to have significantly higher homicide rates, while Hindu and Muslim countries seem to have lower homicide rates than the average, even after controlling for other possible determinants of crime rates. Of the regional dummies, South and East Asian countries seem to have significantly lower homicide rates than the average, while Latin America seems to have higher rates than the average.[15]

Table 3 reports the cross-sectional regression results for the incidence of robberies. As mentioned, these results should be interpreted with caution given that the robbery rates may suffer from under-reporting more severely than the intentional homicide rates.

The results of the robbery regressions are in several respects similar to those for the homicide rate. The level of per capita income is not a significant determinant of robbery rates, but a worsening of income inequality is statistically related to higher robbery rates. However, the drug producers dummy appears to be less important in the robbery regressions than in the homicide regressions. The coefficient of the secondary enrollment rate is also positive in regression (3), and is actually more significant than in the corresponding homicide regression. However, the deterrence and incapacitation variables appear with noticeably different coefficients in the robbery regressions. First, the presence of police personnel variable turns out to have a positive and significant coefficient, which may reflect that police presence is endogenous. The conviction and death penalty variables introduced in regression (5) and (6) appear with the expected negative signs, but neither is statistically significant.

An interesting result, that contrasts with those of the homicide regressions, is that the urbanization rate seems to have a positive and significant association with the robbery rate; the coefficient is significant in 14 of the 16 specifications. This result may indicate that this type of crime may be related to population density and the social interactions that arise from it. As in the homicide regression, the index of ethno-linguistic fractionalization is also not a significant determinant of robbery rates. Regarding the religion and regional dummy variables, the results reported in Table 3 are consistent with the results in Table 2, but with the additional finding that Sub-Saharan African countries also tend to have a significantly higher robbery rate than the average.

B. PANEL REGRESSIONS

1. Methodology

The cross-sectional results emphasize the cross-country variation of crime rates and their determinants. However, further analysis is possible given that the available data on crime rates and their determinants allow the use of an unbalanced panel with five-year periods. The time-series dimension of the data can add important information and permit a richer model specification. First, we would like to test whether the crime rate varies along the business cycle by including the five-year average GDP growth rate in the regression model; this test could not be done using cross-sectional data averaged over a long period of time (1970–94). Second, we would like to test whether there is inertia in crime rates, by including the lagged crime rate in the model. Third, we would like to control for the likely joint endogeneity of some of the explanatory variables and the bias due to under-reporting. And, fourth, we would like to control for the presence of unobserved country-specific effects.

Our preferred panel estimation strategy follows the Generalized Method of Moments (GMM) estimator proposed by Chamberlain (1984), Holtz-Eakin, Newey and Rosen (1988), Arellano and Bond (1991), and Arellano and Bover (1995), which has been applied to cross-country studies by Caselli, Esquivel and Lefort (1996) and Easterly, Loayza and Montiel (1997). The following is a brief presentation of the GMM estimator to be used.[16]

We will work under two econometric models. In the first one, we assume that there are no unobserved country-specific effects. In the second one, we allow and control for them. Why do we also work with the constrained model of no country-specific effects? The data requirements to handle appropriately the presence of country-specific effects (namely, a minimum of three consecutive observations per country in the sample) produce the loss of a large amount of observations in our panel, which is of rather limited coverage to start with. Considering the model without country-specific effects increases the number of observations at the cost of estimating a more restricted model.

a. Assuming no unobserved country-specific effects

Consider the following regression equation,

$$y_{i,t} = \alpha y_{i,t-1} + \beta X_{i,t} + \epsilon_{i,t} \qquad \textbf{(8)}$$

where y represents a crime rate, x represents the set of explanatory variables other than the lagged crime rate, ϵ is the error term, and the subscripts i and t represent country and time period, respectively.

We would like to relax the assumption that all the explanatory variables are strictly exogenous (that is, that they are uncorrelated with the error term at all leads and lags). Relaxing this assumption allows for the possibility of simultaneity and reverse causality, which are very likely present in crime regressions. We adopt the assumption of weak exogeneity of at least some of the explanatory variables, in the sense that they are assumed to be uncorrelated with future realizations of the error term. For example, in the case of reverse causality this weaker assumption means that current explanatory variables may be affected by past and current crime rates but not by future crime rates. In practice we assume that all variables are weakly exogenous except for the drug producers dummy and the GDP growth rate.

Furthermore, we would like to allow and control for the possibility that errors in the measurement of the crime rate (which are imbedded in the error term ϵ) be correlated with some of the explanatory variables. This would be the case if, for instance, the degree of crime under-reporting decreases with the population's level of education. As explained below, our method of estimation corrects this type of mis-measurement bias, as long as the error in measurement is not serially correlated.

Under the assumption that the error *term,* ϵ, is not serially correlated, the assumption of weak exogeneity of the explanatory variables implies the following moment conditions,

$$E\,[X_{i,t-s} \bullet \epsilon_{i,t}] = 0 \text{ for } s \geq 1 \qquad \textbf{(9)}$$

These moment conditions mean that the observations of X lagged one or more periods are valid instruments for the corresponding contemporaneous observations.

Given that the lagged crime rate is also measured with error, it must also be replaced by an instrument. Again, under the assumption that ϵ is not serially correlated, observations of the crime rate lagged two or more periods are valid instruments for the lagged crime rate, y_{t-1}. That is, the following moment conditions apply,

$$E[y_{i,t-s} \bullet \epsilon_{i,t}] = 0 \text{ for } s \geq 2 \qquad \textbf{(10)}$$

b. Allowing and controlling for unobserved country-specific effects

Consider the following regression equation,

$$y_{i,t} = \alpha y_{i,t-1} + \beta X_{i,t} + \eta_i + \epsilon_{i,t} \qquad \textbf{(11)}$$

Equation (11) differs from (8) in that it includes η_i, an unobserved country-specific effect. The usual method to deal with the specific effect in the context of panel data has been to first-difference the regression equation (Anderson and Hsiao 1981). In this way the specific-effect is directly eliminated from the estimation process. First-differencing equation (11), we obtain

$$y_{i,t} - y_{i,t-1} = \alpha(y_{i,t-1} - y_{i,t-2}) + \beta\,(X_{i,t} - X_{i,t-1}) + (\epsilon_{i,t} - \epsilon_{i,t-1}) \qquad \textbf{(12)}$$

The use of instruments is again required to deal with several problems: first, the likely joint endogeneity of the explanatory variables, X; second, the fact that mis-measurement in the contemporaneous crime rate may be correlated with the explanatory variables; third, the fact that the lagged crime rate is likely to be measured with error; and fourth, the fact that by differencing, we introduce by construction a correlation between the new error term, $\epsilon_{i,t} - \epsilon_{i,t-1}$, and the differenced lagged dependent variable, $y_{i,t-1} - y_{i,t-2}$. Under the assumption that the error term ϵ is not serially correlated, the following moment conditions apply in relation to, respectively, the lagged dependent variable and the set of explanatory variables,

$$E\,[y_{i,t-s} \bullet (\epsilon_{i,t} - \epsilon_{i,t-1})] = 0 \text{ for } s \geq 3 \qquad \textbf{(13)}$$

$$E\,[X_{i,t-s} \bullet (\epsilon_{i,t} - \epsilon_{i,t-1})] = 0 \text{ for } s \geq 2 \qquad \textbf{(14)}$$

Arellano and Bond (1991) develop a consistent GMM estimator based on moment conditions similar to those in equations (13) and (14). However, for reasons explained below, we will use an estimator that complements these moment conditions (applied to the regression in differences) with appropriate moment conditions applied to the regression in *levels*. Before explaining the statistical advantages of the estimator that combines differences and levels regressions over the simple difference estimator, a conceptual justification for our approach is the following: This paper studies not only the time-series determinants of crime rates but also their cross-country variation, which is eliminated in the case of the simple difference estimator.

Alonso-Borrego and Arellano (1996) and Blundell and Bond (1997) show that when the lagged dependent and the explanatory variables are persistent over time, lagged levels of these variables are weak instruments for the regression equation in differences. The instruments' weakness has repercussions on both the asymptotic and small-sample performance of the difference estimator. As the variables' persistence increases, the asymptotic variance of the coefficients obtained with the difference estimator rises (that is, the asymptotic precision of this estimator deteriorates). Furthermore, Monte Carlo experiments show that the weakness of the instruments produces biased coefficients in small samples; this bias is exacerbated with the variables' over time persistence, the importance of the specific-effect, and the smallness of the time-series dimension. An additional problem with the simple difference estimator relates to measurement error: Differencing may exacerbate the bias due to errors in variables by decreasing the signal-to-noise ratio (see Griliches and Hausman, 1986).

On the basis of both asymptotic and small-sample properties, Blundell and Bond (1997) suggest the use of the Arellano and Bover (1995) estimator in place of the usual difference estimator. Arellano and Bover (1995) present an estimator that combines, in a system, the regression in differences with the regression in levels. The instruments for the regression in differences are the lagged *levels* of the corresponding variables; therefore, the moment conditions in equations (13) and (14) apply to this first part of the system. The instruments for the regression in levels are the lagged *differences* of the corresponding variables. These are appropriate instruments under the following two assumptions: First, the error term ϵ is not serially correlated. And second, although there may be correlation between the levels of the right-hand side variables and the country-specific effect, there is no correlation between the *differences* of these variables and the specific effect. The second assumption results from the following stationarity property,

$$E[y_{i,t+p} \bullet \eta_i] = E[y_{i,t+q} \bullet \eta_i] \text{ and } E[X_{i,t+p} \bullet \eta_i] = E[X_{i,t+q} \bullet \eta_i] \text{ for all } p \text{ and } q \quad \textbf{(15)}$$

Therefore, the moment conditions for the second part of the system (the regression in levels) are given by,

$$E[(y_{i,t-s} - y_{i,t-s-1}) \bullet (\eta_i + \epsilon_{i,t})] = 0 \text{ for } s \geq 2 \quad \textbf{(16)}$$

$$E[(X_{i,t-s} - X_{i,t-s-1}) \bullet (\eta_i + \epsilon_{i,t})] = 0 \text{ for } s \geq 1 \quad \textbf{(17)}$$

2. Summary of the methodology

The estimation strategy proposed in this paper can deal with unobserved fixed effects in a dynamic (lagged-dependent variable) model, joint endogeneity of the explanatory variables, and serially-uncorrelated crime rate mis-measurement. The moment conditions presented above can be used in the context of the Generalized Method of Moments (GMM) to generate consistent and efficient estimates of the parameters of interest (Arellano and Bond, 1991; and Arellano and Bover, 1995). Specifically, in the model that ignores unobserved country-specific effects, the moment conditions in equations (9) and (10) are used; and in the model that allows and controls for unobserved specific effects, the moment conditions in equations (13), (14), (16), and (17) are used.[17]

The consistency of the GMM estimator depends on whether lagged values of the crime rate and the other explanatory variables are valid instruments in the crime regression. To address this issue we present two specification test, suggested by Arellano and Bond (1991). The first is a Sargan test of over-identifying restrictions, which tests the overall validity of the instruments by analyzing the sample analog of the moment conditions used in the estimation process. The second test examines the hypothesis that the error term $\epsilon_{i,t}$ is not serially correlated. In the levels regression we test whether the error term is first- or second-order serially correlated, and in the system difference-level regression we test whether the differenced error term is second-order serially correlated (by construction, it is likely that this differenced error term be first-order serially correlated even if the original error term is not). Under both tests, failure to reject the null hypothesis gives support to the model.

3. Results

Table 4 reports the results of GMM panel regressions for the intentional homicide rate, both ignoring and controlling for unobserved country-specific effects. It must be noted that, given that we are controlling for possible problems of simultaneity and reverse causality, we can interpret the estimated coefficients not simply as partial associations but as effects of the explanatory variables on homicide rates. As in the cross-sectional regressions, we consider a "core" set of explanatory variables consisting of the GDP growth rate, the (log) of GNP per capita, the Gini index, the average years of schooling of the population older than 15 years of age, the urbanization rate, a dummy for whether the country produces illegal drugs, the drug possession crimes rate, and (except for the first regression) the lagged homicide rate. To this core set, we add in turn the secondary enrollment rate, the ratio of policemen per inhabitant in the country, and the homicide conviction rate.

Table 4. GMM Panel Regressions of the Log of Intentional Homicide Rates
(p-values in parenthesis)

	(1)	*(2)*	*(3)*	*(4)*	*(5)*
Regression Specification	*Levels*				
Instruments (*)	*Levels*				
GDP Growth Rate	-0.101 (0.000)	-0.064 (0.000)	-0.056 (0.000)	-0.047 (0.000)	-0.034 (0.011)
Log of GNP per Capita	-0.305 (0.161)	0.026 (0.588)	0.017 (0.740)	-0.049 (0.039)	-0.021 (0.748)
Gini Index	0.034 (0.060)	0.021 (0.000)	0.016 (0.000)	0.016 (0.001)	0.012 (0.117)
Average Years of Schooling	0.007 (0.923)	0.015 (0.591)		-0.073 (0.000)	0.011 (0.848)
Urbanization Rate	-0.000 (0.971)	-0.002 (0.216)	-0.002 (0.143)	0.003 (0.095)	-0.003 (0.378)
Drug Producers Dummy	0.196 (0.564)	0.338 (0.006)	0.238 (0.000)	0.311 (0.000)	0.648 (0.000)
Drug Possession Crimes Rate	0.004 (0.000)	0.001 (0.058)	0.001 (0.074)	0.002 (0.000)	0.001 (0.259)
Lagged Homicide Rate		0.737 (0.000)	0.761 (0.000)	0.723 (0.000)	0.570 (0.000)
Secondary Enrollment Rate			0.000 (0.912)		
Police				-0.000 (0.019)	
Conviction Rate					-0.006 (0.009)
Constant	2.354 (0.175)	-0.478 (0.154)	-0.117 (0.668)	0.581 (0.042)	0.631 (0.349)
Sargan Test of Overidentifying Restrictions: p-value	0.545	0.397	0.511	0.365	0.369
Test for First-Order Serial Correlation: p -value	0.000	0.530	0.879	0.647	0.888
Test for Second-Order Serial Correlation: p -value	0.006	0.911	0.202	0.284	0.550
Number of Observations (Countries)	153 (68)	85 (45)	76 (42)	49 (27)	31 (21)

The first regression in Table 4 considers a static specification (that is, one excluding the lagged crime rate as explanatory variable). This specification is rejected by the error serial-correlation tests; therefore, its estimated coefficients cannot offer valid conclusions. The correlation of the error term in this regression signals that relevant variables with high over-time persistence were omitted; these variables can be the lagged homicide rate (which makes the model dynamic) and/or the country-specific effect. When the lagged homicide rate is included in subsequent regressions, both the hypothesis of lack of residual serial correlation and the hypothesis of no correlation between the error term and the instruments (Sargan test) cannot be rejected, and,

Table 4. Continued

	(6)	*(7)*	*(8)*
Regression Specification	*Levels*	*Dif.-Lev.*	
Instruments (*)	*Levels*	*Lev. Dif.*	
GDP Growth Rate	-0.052 (0.000)	-0.051 (0.000)	-0.036 (0.001)
Log of GNP per Capita	-0.046 (.343)	-0.014 (0.289)	-0.207 (0.000)
Gini Index	0.008 (0.335)	0.021 (0.000)	0.036 (0.000)
Average Years of Schooling	0.023 (0.257)	-0.040 (0.001)	
Urbanization Rate	-0.002 (0.340)	0.004 (0.130)	0.004 (0.063)
Drug Producers Dummy	0.246 (0.135)		
Drug Possession Crimes Rate	0.001 (0.083)	0.000 (0.299)	0.001 (0.047)
Lagged Homicide Rate	0.893 (0.000)	0.664 (0.000)	0.640 (0.000)
Secondary Enrollment Rate	0.009 (0.000)		
1980–84 Period Dummy	-0.036 (0.530)		
1985–89 Period Dummy	0.071 (0.299)		
1990–94 Period Dummy	0.141 (0.051)		
Constant	0.322 (.468)		
Sargan Test of Overidentifying Restrictions: p-value	0.397	0.589	0.839
Test for First-Order Serial Correlation: p-value	0.357	0.278	0.278
Test for Second-Order Serial Correlation: p-value	0.767	0.280	0.319
Number of Observations (Countries)	86 (46)	60 (22)	54 (20)

(*) In the levels specification, all variables are assumed to be only weakly exogenous, except for the GDP growth rate and the drug producers dummy, which are assumed to be strictly exogenous. The second lag is used as an instrument for the lagged crime rate. As for the other variables, the instrument used is the first lag. The only exception to the previous rule is regression (4), where the Gini index and the urbanization rate are assumed to be strictly exogenous due to limitations in the sample size. In the specification that includes both differences and levels, the lagged first differences are used as instruments in the equations in levels, with the exception of the lagged crime rate for which we use the second lag of the first difference, and the GDP growth rate, which is assumed to be strictly exogenous. In the equations in differences, all first differences are assumed to be strictly exogenous, except for the lagged first difference of the crime rate, which is instrumented with the third lag of the crime rate (in level). Standard errors are adjusted for heteroskedasticity.

thus, the dynamic model is supported by the specification tests. The dynamic model with country-specific effects (regressions (7) and (8)) is also supported by the Sargan and second-order serial correlation tests.

From the regressions ignoring country-specific effects (regressions (2) to (6)) and those accounting for them (regressions (7) and (8)), the most robust and significant results in relation to the core variables are the following: First, the business cycle effect, measured by the coefficient on GDP growth rate holding constant average per capita income, is statistically significant and shows that, as expected, crime is counter-cyclical; stagnant economic activity induces heightened homicide rates. Second, higher income inequality, measured by the Gini index, increases the incidence of homicide rates; this result survives the inclusion of lagged homicide rates and is strengthened when unobserved country-specific effects are taken into account. The only regression where the Gini coefficient loses its statistical significance is the one that allows for time-specific effects. In addition, the combination of significant effects of the business cycle and income distribution tells us that the rate of poverty reduction may be associated with declines in crime rates.[18] Third, higher drug related activity, represented by both drug production and drug possession, induces a higher incidence of intentional homicide. It must be noted that the drug producers dummy loses some of its significance when time effects are allowed, and the drug possession crimes rate is not robustly significant when country-specific effects are accounted for. Fourth, the lagged homicide rate has a positive and significant impact on current rates, which is evidence of criminal inertia, as predicted by recent crime theoretical models. The size of the coefficient on the lagged homicide rate decreases but remains significant when country-specific effects are controlled for, which indicates that country-specific factors explain only a portion of criminal inertia.

As in the cross-sectional regressions, the level of income per capita does not have an independent, significant effect on the homicide rate. The results concerning the urbanization rate are not robust to the issue of country-specific effects. In the model without country-specific effects, the urbanization rate does not affect significantly the homicide rate. However, when country-specific effects are controlled for, the urbanization rate is associated with larger homicide rates.[19]

The puzzle concerning the lack of a significantly negative association between a country's educational stand and its homicide rate is somewhat clarified in the panel regressions that account for country-specific effects. When a country's educational stand is proxied by the secondary enrollment rate, its effect on homicide rates is significantly positive.[20] However, when the average years of schooling in the adult population is used to proxy for the country's educational position, it has a significant crime-reducing impact. The contrast between the results obtained using secondary enrollment rates and average years of schooling may indicate that the efforts to educate the young may not reduce crime immediately but eventually lead to a reduction of crime, especially of the violent sort.

In regressions (4) and (5) we examine the effect of the strength of the police and judicial system in deterring crime. The proxies we use are, in turn, the rate of policemen per inhabitant in the country and the homicide conviction rate. Both variables are subject to joint endogeneity in crime regressions, and the conviction rate may be spuriously negatively correlated with the homicide rate given the mis-measurement in the number of homicides. Because of these reasons, the panel GMM estimator is clearly superior to the cross-sectional results. Since we are instrumenting for both the policemen rate and the conviction rate (and the specification tests support the model), we conclude that the negative and significant coefficient on both proxies means that a stronger police and judicial system does lead to a lower incidence of homicides.

In regression (6) we examine the importance of time-specific effects. We find that in the period 1990–94, the world has experienced a statistically significant increase in homicide rates relative to those in the late 1970s and early 1980s; this rise in homicide rates cannot be fully

Table 5. GMM Panel Regressions of the Log of Robbery Rates
(p-values in parenthesis)

	(1)	(2)	(3)	(4)
Regression Specification	*Levels*		*Dif.-Lev.*	
Instruments (*)	*Levels*		*Lev.-Dif.*	
GDP Growth Rate	-0.069	-0.096	-0.091	-0.072
	(0.009)	(0.000)	(0.000)	(0.000)
Log of GNP per Capita	0.533	0.162	0.038	-0.045
	(0.076)	(0.017)	(0.219)	(0.035)
Gini Index	0.137	0.038	0.006	0.011
	(0.000)	(0.000)	(0.003)	(0.009)
Average Years of Schooling	-0.010	0.031	-0.025	
	(0.866)	(0.045)	(0.093)	
Urbanization Rate	-0.000	-0.005	0.008	0.011
	(0.980)	(0.038)	(0.000)	(0.000)
Drug Producers Dummy	0.625	-0.478		
	(0.053)	(0.000)		
Drug Possession Crimes Rate	0.007	0.000	0.001	0.001
	(0.000)	(0.879)	(0.012)	(0.019)
Lagged Robbery Rate		0.891	0.833	0.839
		(0.000)	(0.000)	(0.000)
Secondary Enrollment Rate				0.002
				(0.191)
Constant	-6.683	-1.791		
	(0.013)	(0.008)		
Sargan Test of Overidentifying Restrictions: p-value	0.156	0.339	0.611	0.628
Test for First-Order Serial Correlations: p-value	0.004	0.091	0.057	0.053
Test for Second-Order Serial Correlation: p value	0.045	0.313	0.760	0.539
Number of Observations (Countries)	133 (56)	77 (39)	58 (20)	50 (17)

(*) In the levels specification, all variables are assumed to be only weakly exogenous, except for the GDP growth rate and the drug producers dummy, which are assumed to be strictly exogenous. The second lag is used as an instrument for the lagged crime rate. As for the other variables, the instrument used is the first lag. In the specification that includes both differences and levels, the lagged first differences are used as instruments in the equations in levels, with the exception of the lagged crime rate for which we use the second lag of the first difference, and the GDP growth rate, which is assumed to be strictly exogenous. In the equations in differences, all first differences are assumed to be strictly exogenous, except for the lagged first difference of the crime rate, which is instrumented with the third lag of the crime rate (in level). In regression (4), the Gini index is also assumed to be strictly exogenous due to limitations in the sample size.

explained by the evolution of the crime determinants in the core model.

Table 5 shows the panel GMM results for the robbery rate. The model specification without a lagged dependent variable or a country-specific effect is strongly rejected by the residual serial correlation tests. In contrast to the homicide regressions, the dynamic specification of the crime regression that ignores country-specific effects is also rejected by the residual serial correlation test. Therefore, we must base our conclusions on the dynamic specification that accounts for specific effects. This prevents us from analyzing the role of the proxies for the strength of the police and judicial system given that the inclusion of these variables limits dramatically the sample size available for estimation of the specific-effect model.

The results of the dynamic model that controls for country-specific effects for the robbery rate are virtually the same as the corresponding ones for the homicide rate[21]: Stagnant economic activity (low GDP growth) promotes heightened robbery rates; the counter cyclical behavior of the robbery rate appears to be larger than that in the case of the homicide rate. Larger income inequality (high Gini index) induces an increase in the incidence of robberies, but not to the same extent as in the case of homicide rate. The robbery rate exhibits a significant degree of inertia, which is somewhat larger than that of the homicide rate. The urbanization rate has a significant positive impact on the incidence of robberies; this impact appears to be larger than in the case of homicides. Although the secondary enrollment rate has a puzzling positive effect on robbery rates, the level of educational attainment of the adult population has a robbery-reducing impact. The drug possession crimes rate is positively associated with the robbery rate. Finally, as in the homicide regressions, the level of per capita income does not appear to be robustly correlated with the robbery rate.

CONCLUSIONS

THE CONCLUSIONS THAT CAN BE DERIVED from the theoretical model and the empirical findings regarding potentially fruitful directions for future research and possible policy implications fall under two headings: the good news and the bad news.

The bad news first. Some bad news is related to the results of the dynamic panel estimation methods (GMM). The results show that economic downturns and other non-economic shocks, such as a rise in drug trafficking, as in Colombia in the 1970s, can raise the national crime rate. The econometric results also suggest that the rise in the crime rate may be felt long after the initial shock—countries can be engulfed in a crime wave. The policy implication of this finding is that policy-makers should act to counter the crime wave, if not, a country may get stuck at an excessively high crime rate.

Although we do not know the precise channels through which a crime shock tends to be perpetuated over time, the existing literature proposes three possible channels: systemic interactions, local interactions, and recidivism. Future research should attempt to clarify which one of these is at work, but this research would probably need to rely on individual-level analysis, because local interactions and recidivism are forces that are determined by an individual's location with respect to her local community and her past criminal record, respectively.

The good news. Two important determinants of crime rates—inequality and deterrence—are, we believe, "policy-sensitive" variables. Policy-makers facing a crime wave should then consider a combination of counter-cyclical re-distributive policies (e.g., targeted safety nets) and increases in the resources devoted to apprehending and convicting criminals—a *"carrots-and-sticks"* policy response would seem to be appropriate, especially during economic recessions. Regarding the crime-inducing effect of inequality, our empirical findings suggest that there is, "a social incentive for equalizing training and earning opportunities across persons, which is independent of ethical considerations or any social welfare function" (Ehrlich 1973, 561). In addition, our empirical findings regarding criminal inertia imply that current crime rates respond to current policy variables with a lag. Sah (1991, 1292) observed that, "This apparent lack of response is a source of frustration for politicians as well as for law enforcement officials... Such reactions, though understandable, may be inappropriate if they are caused by an inadequate understanding of the dynamics of crime."

Future research in this area should attempt to solve the crime-education puzzle present in our empirical findings. We have provided a result which may prove to be one of the clues to solve the puzzle: there is a delayed effect of educational effort on crime alleviation, that is, the crime-reducing effect of education does not materialize when the young are being educated but mostly when they become adults. Another clue to the puzzle may be obtained by considering the indirect effects of education on inequality.

This paper was motivated by the impression that crime has pernicious effects on economic activity, and may also reduce welfare by reducing individuals sense of personal and proprietary security. Indeed, a fertile area for future research is to attempt to measure the effects of criminal behavior on economic growth and welfare. We suspect that there are many ways of measuring the economic costs of crime, ranging from the costs of maintaining an effective police and judicial system, to estimates of the forgone output. However, the overall effects on welfare may be more difficult to assess.

APPENDIX: DATA DESCRIPTION AND SOURCES

THIS APPENDIX PRESENTS the data used in this paper, with special attention to the variables related with crime rates, conviction rates and police personnel. Table A1 provides the description and sources of all the variables that were used. References are provided for details on the variables that have been previously used in other academic papers. In the case of the crime-related data, even though the information that was used is publicly available, additional work was required in order to assemble the variables actually used in the econometric estimations.

These variables were constructed with information provided by the United Nations, through its Crime Prevention and Criminal Justice Division. The United Nations has conducted, since 1978, five Surveys of Crime Trends and Operations of Criminal Justice Systems. Each survey has covered periods of five to six years, requesting crime data from government officials covering the period from 1970 to 1994. The statistics included in these surveys represent the official statistics of member countries of the United Nations. They have been compiled by the United Nations on the basis of questionnaires distributed to member countries, as well as yearbooks, annual reports, and statistical abstracts of these countries. The United Nations Surveys are available on the internet at http://www.ifs.univie.ac.at/~uncjin/wcs.html#wcs123.

In order to construct series covering the period 1970–94 for the largest number of countries, the five U.N. Surveys were used. When these surveys overlap (in 1975, 1980, 1986 and 1990), the information from the latest survey was used. It is worth noting that most of the countries did not respond to all surveys, so that missing values are a common occurrence in these series. The definitions of the various crimes are stable across the surveys and are detailed in Table A1. However, as stated by Newman and DiCristina (1992), who constructed a data set with the information of the first and second surveys, the definitions "were applied as far as possible." Moreover, they add, "it will be recognized that, owing to the immense variation in criminal justice systems around the world, these categories are of necessity rough" (Newman and DiCristina 1992, 6).

In addition to assembling the series for the yearly number of crimes and convictions in each country, we conducted a "cleaning" of the data. This process, inherently based on arbitrary judgments, was nonetheless guided by the following criteria. We analyzed the evolution of the variables over time, searching for large and discontinuous changes. More specifically, we looked for situations where a change in the order of magnitude of the variables (e.g., ten-fold or hundred-fold increases) occurred from one survey to the other. In the cases where it was apparent that, in each new survey, the level of a specific variable experienced this type of abrupt and permanent change, all the observations for the corresponding country and variable were dropped for the period in question. This decision was based on the assumption that these changes could only be explained by changes in the definitions or criteria used in the collection of the data by the respondents of the corresponding questionnaires. In addition, when these definition changes were apparent in only one small subperiod (e.g., corresponding to only one survey or subperiod thereof) this subperiod was dropped for the corresponding country and variable.

Table A1. Description and Source of the Variables

Variable	*Description*	*Source*
Intentional Homicide Rate	Death purposely inflicted by another person, per 100,000 population.	Constructed from the United Nations World Crime Surveys of Crime Trends and Operations of Criminal Justice Systems, various issues, except for Argentina, Brazil, Colombia, Mexico, and Venezuela. The data is available on the internet at http://www.ifs.univie.ac.at/~uncjin/wcs.html#wcs123. The data on population was taken from the World Bank's International Economic Department database. For the five Latin American countries listed above, the source for the number of homicides was the Health Situation Analysis Program of the Division of Health and Human Development, Pan-American Health Organization, from the PAHO Technical Information System. This source provided us with data on the annual number of deaths attributed to homicides, which come from national vital statistics systems.
Robbery Rate	Total number of robberies recorded by the police, per 100,000 population. Robbery refers to the taking away of property from a person, overcoming resistance by force or threat of force.	Same as above.
Conviction Rates (of Intentional Homicides, Theft, Robbery, and Assault)	The number of persons found guilty of a specific crime (intentional homicides, theft, robbery, or assault) by any legal body duly authorized to do so under national law, divided by the total number of the corresponding crime (in percentage).	Same as above.
Police	Number of police personnel per 100,000 population.	Same as above.
Drug Possession Crime Rate	Number of drug possession offenses per 100,000 population.	Same as above.
Drug Producers Dummy	Dummy that takes the value one for the countries which are considered significant producers of illicit drugs.	International Narcotics Control Strategy Report, U.S. Department of State, Bureau for International Narcotics and Law Enforcement Affairs, various issues.

Table A1. Continued

Variable	Description	Source
Gini Index	Gini Coefficient, after adding 6.6 to the expenditure-based data to make it comparable to the income-based data.	Constructed from Deininger and Squire (1996). The dataset is available on the internet from the World Bank's Server, at http://www.worldbank.org/html/prdmg/grthweb/datasets.htm.
Average Years of Schooling	Average years of schooling of the population over 15.	Barro and Lee (1996). The dataset is available on the internet from the World Bank's Server, at http:// www.worldbank.org/html/prdmg/grthweb/datasets.htm.
Secondary Enrollment	Ratio of total enrollment, regardless of age, to the population of the age group that officially corresponds to the secondary level of education.	World Bank, International Economic Department data base.
GNP per capita	Gross National Product expressed in constant 1987 U.S. dollars.	Same as above.
Growth of GDP	Growth in the Gross Domestic Product expressed in constant 1987 local currency prices.	Same as above.
Urbanization Rate	Percentage of the total population living in urban agglomerations.	Same as above.
Political Assassinations Rate	Number of political assassinations per 100,000 population.	Easterly and Levine (1997). The dataset is available on the internet from the World Bank's Server, at http://www.worldbank.org/html/prdmg/grthweb/datasets.htm.
Dummy for War on National Territory	Dummy for war on national territory during the decade of 1970 or 1980.	Same as above.
Absence of Corruption Index	ICRG index of corruption in government, ranging from 1 to 6, with higher ratings indicating few ethical problems in conducting business.	International Country Risk Guide.
Rule of Law Index	ICRG measure of law and order tradition, ranging from 1 to 6, with lower ratings indicating a tradition of depending on physical force or illegal means to settle claims, as opposed to a reliance on established institutions and laws.	Same as above.
Index of Ethno-Linguistic Fractionalization	Measure that two randomly selected people from a given country will not belong to the same ethno-linguistic group (1960).	Easterly and Levine (1997). The dataset is available on the internet from the World Bank's Server, at http://www.worldbank.org/html/prdmg/grthweb/datasets.htm.
Buddhist Dummy	Dummy for countries where Buddhism is the religion with the largest number of followers.	CIA Factbook. The data is available on the internet at http://www.odci.gov/cia/publications/pubs.html.
Christian Dummy	Dummy for countries where Christian religions are the ones with the largest number of followers.	Same as above.

Table A1. Continued

Variable	Description	Source
Hindu Dummy	Dummy for countries where Hinduism is the religion with the largest number of followers.	Same as above.
Muslim Dummy	Dummy for countries where Islam is the religion with the largest number of followers.	Same as above.
Africa Dummy	Dummy for Developing Countries of Sub-Saharan Africa.	Classification used in the Data Bases of the World Bank International Economic Department.
Asia Dummy	Dummy for Developing Countries of Asia.	Same as above.
Europe and Central Asia Dummy	Dummy for Developing Countries of Europe and Central Asia.	Same as above.
Latin America Dummy	Dummy for Developing Countries of Latin America.	Same as above.
Middle East Dummy	Dummy for Developing Countries of the Middle East and Northern Africa.	Same as above.
Africa and Latin America Dummy	Dummy for Developing Countries of Africa and Latin America.	Same as above.
Index of Firearm Regulations	Measure of restrictions affecting ownership, importing, and mobility of hand guns and long guns in the early 1990s. Weights of .5, .25 and .25 were given to the resulting measures (2 given to country if it prohibits or restricts all firearms; 1 given to country if it prohibits or restricts some firearms; 0 given to country if it does not have either prohibitions or restrictions on firearms) regarding ownership, imports, and movement, respectively.	United Nations International Study on Firearm Regulation at http://www.ifs.univie.ac.at/~uncjin/firearms/.
Alcohol Consumption	Annual alcohol consumption per capita in liters, covering the period 1982–91.	Alcoholism and Drug Addiction Research Foundation (Toronto, Ontario, Canada) in collaboration with the Programme on Substance Abuse of the World Health Organization. International Profile: Alcohol & Other Drugs, 1994.
Death Penalty	Dummy for countries whose laws do (1) or do not (0) provide for the death penalty. Some countries experienced changes, either abolishing or imposing the death penalty during 1970-94. Hence period averages range between 0 and 1.	Amnesty International. List of Abolitionist and Retentionist Countries at http://www.amnesty.org/ailib/intcam/dp/abrelist.htm#7
Ratio of Males Aged 15 to 29 (34) to Total Population	Ratio of number of males aged 15 to 29 (34) to total population.	Pre-formatted projection tables in the World Development Indicators database of the World Bank.

Table A2. Summary Statistics of Intentional Homicide Rates by Country

(Annual Data)

Country	No. of Obs.	Mean	Standard Deviation	Min.	Max.	First Year	Last Year
Industrialized and High-Income Developing Countries							
Australia	22	2.432	0.728	1.586	3.789	1970	1994
Austria	25	2.332	0.339	1.804	3.191	1970	1994
The Bahamas	22	27.950	20.587	6.322	83.088	1970	1994
Belgium	3	3.010	0.323	2.648	3.268	1983	1994
Bermuda	15	4.403	5.182	0.000	17.036	1980	1994
Canada	22	2.355	0.247	0.633	2.732	1970	1994
Cyprus	25	3.551	4.407	0.633	15.902	1970	1994
Denmark	25	3.706	1.939	0.507	6.013	1970	1994
Finland	20	5.445	2.568	2.192	10.061	1975	1994
France	17	3.348	1.963	0.400	4.937	1970	1994
Germany	21	3.432	0.231	3.045	3.886	1970	1990
Hong Kong, China	12	1.794	0.339	1.285	2.454	1980	1994
Israel	15	4.841	1.089	2.210	6.286	1975	1994
Italy	25	4.151	1.353	2.293	7.284	1970	1994
Japan	25	1.489	0.361	0.980	2.106	1970	1994
Kuwait	23	5.447	3.163	0.879	11.814	1970	1994
Luxembourg	2	7.586	0.011	7.578	7.594	1986	1990
Netherlands	16	11.115	2.476	7.303	15.994	1975	1990
New Zealand	17	1.201	0.502	0.586	2.411	1970	1986
Norway	21	0.959	0.618	0.205	2.546	1970	1990
Portugal	14	4.165	0.628	2.559	4.873	1977	1990
Qatar	25	2.100	0.767	1.103	3.674	1970	1994
Singapore	25	2.400	0.596	1.526	3.828	1970	1994
Spain	23	1.956	1.463	0.083	5.010	1970	1994
Sweden	25	4.06	2.885	1.243	9.532	1970	1994
Switzerland	18	1.883	0.899	0.395	3.188	1970	1994
United Arab Emirates	6	3.589	1.013	2.325	5.149	1975	1980
United Kingdom	15	1.920	0.394	1.481	2.566	1970	1986
United States	22	8.386	1.096	6.436	10.105	1970	1994
Latin America and the Caribbean							
Antigua & Barbuda	2	7.238	1.168	6.412	8.065	1985	1986
Argentina	18	5.159	1.347	3.489	9.079	1970	1993
Barbados	16	5.909	2.317	2.893	11.664	1970	1990
Belize	6	21.506	5.567	12.623	25.647	1975	1980
Brazil	16	14.497	4.270	7.699	21.614	1977	1992
Chile	16	5.662	3.049	2.206	14.127	1970	1994
Colombia	19	44.962	26.634	13.895	86.044	1970	1994
Costa Rica	18	9.218	5.120	3.779	19.122	1970	1994
Cuba	7	4.248	1.585	3.176	7.718	1970	1977
Dominica	7	0.080	0.0132	0.032	0.120	1980	1986
Ecuador	9	7.156	6.559	0.325	17.930	1970	1994
El Salvador	4	25.304	7.083	15.024	30.213	1970	1973
Guyana	7	7.873	1.257	6.939	10.426	1970	1976
Honduras	12	7.110	3.087	3.327	13.326	1975	1986
Jamaica	20	19.536	7.949	7.596	41.678	1970	1994
Mexico	25	18.037	2.019	12.723	22.419	1970	1994
Nicaragua	5	21.297	3.853	15.520	25.376	1990	1994
Panama	6	10.932	2.899	7.590	14.692	1975	1980
Peru	13	2.172	1.212	.035	4.777	1970	1986
St. Kitts & Nevis	9	6.592	3.468	2.347	11.450	1980	1990
St. Lucia	1	3.232	n.a.	3.232	3.232	1980	1980
St. Vincent & the Grenadines	9	14.441	4.505	9.116	20.896	1980	1991
Suriname	9	7.605	9.908	1.089	30.757	1975	1986
Trinidad & Tobago	18	6.786	1.493	4.991	10.357	1970	1990
Uruguay	12	5.376	1.160	3.680	7.367	1980	1994
Venezuela	23	10.017	2.643	7.280	15.833	1970	1994

Table A2. Continued

Country	No. of Obs.	Mean	Standard Deviation	Min.	Max.	First Year	Last Year
Eastern Europe and Central Asia							
Armenia	5	3.002	1.641	1.718	5.726	1986	1990
Azerbaijan	5	7.877	1.194	6.733	9.602	1990	1994
Belarus	5	7.142	1.666	5.316	9.193	1990	1994
Bulgaria	21	5.161	2.413	3.255	10.800	1970	1994
Croatia	5	10.584	3.635	7.283	14.925	1990	1994
Czech Republic	16	1.190	0.306	0.716	2.046	1975	1990
Estonia	5	15.774	7.211	8.685	24.350	1990	1994
Georgia	3	2.610	2.601	0.959	7.216	1990	1994
Gibraltar	8	2.389	3.524	0	2.532	1975	1986
Greece	25	1.466	0.670	0.301	8	1970	1994
Hungary	15	3.853	0.470	2.981	4.517	1980	1994
Kazakstan	9	10.478	3.160	7.020	15.244	1986	1994
Kyrgyz Republic	5	10.912	2.547	8.191	13.720	1990	1994
Latvia	9	8.377	4.738	3.945	16.589	1986	1994
Lithuania	9	7.052	3.966	3.457	14.055	1986	1994
Macedonia	5	0.825	0.293	0.592	1.324	1990	1994
Malta	15	2.047	1.350	0.288	4.428	1980	1994
Moldova	9	7.035	2.242	4.564	11.465	1986	1994
Poland	21	1.660	0.316	1.001	2.327	1970	1990
Romania	9	4.500	1.866	2.194	6.516	1986	1994
Russian Federation	9	11.928	5.738	6.301	21.815	1986	1994
San Marino	6	2.729	4.615	0	11.111	1970	1975
Slovak Republic	5	2.271	0.315	1.760	2.554	1990	1994
Slovenia	9	4.117	0.609	3.181	5.209	1986	1994
Tajikistan	4	2.541	0.462	2.055	3.168	1987	1990
Turkey	6	16.556	1.960	14.090	19.931	1970	1975
Ukraine	15	5.196	1.538	3.439	8.804	1980	1994
Yugoslavia, FR (Serbia)	7	13.007	3.237	10.939	19.934	1975	1990
Middle East and North Africa							
Algeria	6	0.924	0.336	0.524	1.468	1970	1975
Bahrain	15	1.388	1.172	0.382	5.042	1970	1990
Egypt, Arab Rep.	23	2.337	1.023	1.392	4.172	1970	1994
Iraq	9	10.517	2.212	8.076	13.482	1970	1978
Jordan	20	3.352	1.756	1.822	7.038	1975	1994
Lebanon	9	15.495	12.478	4.479	42.898	1970	1988
Morocco	14	1.071	0.386	0.689	2.157	1970	1994
Oman	6	0.824	0.893	0	2.461	1970	1975
Saudi Arabia	10	0.767	0.168	0.519	1.062	1970	1979
Syrian Arab Republic	22	4.083	1.431	1.964	6.263	1970	1994
Sub-Saharan Africa							
Botswana	10	10.179	1.742	6.652	13.031	1980	1990
Burundi	7	1.088	0.164	0.758	1.284	1980	1986
Cape Verde	1	5.242		5.242	5.242	1979	1979
Ethiopia	5	10.185	2.678	5.682	12.298	1986	1990
Liberia	5	2.615	1.635	0.530	5.028	1982	1986
Madagascar	15	6.597	13.327	0.468	53.432	1975	1994
Malawi	7	2.762	0.483	2.059	3.399	1980	1986
Mauritius	15	2.652	0.399	2.081	3.448	1970	1994
SãoTomé and Principe	5	118.429	21.184	90.749	142.014	1990	1994
Senegal	6	2.186	0.277	1.914	2.598	1975	1980
Seychelles	6	4.467	2.234	1.642	8.335	1975	1980
South Africa	6	22.874	4.358	18.249	29.853	1975	1980
Sudan	15	5.406	1.301	3.262	7.045	1970	1994
Swaziland	5	68.048	8.495	58.813	81.738	1986	1990
Zambia	6	8.605	1.293	6.973	10.160	1975	1980
Zimbabwe	10	9.544	4.909	4.336	18.344	1975	1994

Table A2. Continued

Country	No. of Obs.	Mean	Standard Deviation	Min.	Max.	First Year	Last Year
South and East Asia							
Bangladesh	12	2.541	0.392	1.984	3.340	1975	1986
China	5	0.965	0.078	0.867	1.076	1981	1986
Fiji	15	2.635	1.117	0.329	4.670	1970	1986
India	17	4.814	2.200	2.655	8.085	1970	1994
Indonesia	19	0.895	0.212	0.108	1.127	1970	1994
Korea, Rep. of	19	1.444	0.168	1.235	1.834	1970	1994
Malaysia	20	1.883	0.367	1.050	2.397	1970	1994
Maldives	5	1.900	0.983	0.463	3.060	1986	1990
Myanmar	5	0.703	0.091	0.563	0.818	1986	1990
Nepal	13	1.584	0.571	0.387	1.994	1970	1986
Pakistan	11	6.069	0.728	4.661	7.034	1970	1980
Papua New Guinea	2	2.080	0.143	1.979	2.181	1975	1976
Philippines	8	9.509	8.378	2.598	29.355	1970	1980
Sri Lanka	17	12.174	10.007	6.295	48.358	1971	1989
Thailand	12	21.506	11.354	7.556	41.776	1970	1990
Tonga	11	7.519	5.163	1.074	14.286	1975	1990
Vanuatu	4	0.881	0.343	0.678	1.395	1987	1994
Western Samoa	5	1.976	1.266	0.613	3.125	1990	1994

NOTES

[1] See, for example, the attention given to the "rising crime wave" in Latin America and the Caribbean in "Law and Order," *Latin Trade,* June 1997, "Mexico City Crime Alarms Multinationals," *The Wall Street Journal*, October 29, 1996, p. A18, and "Reform Backlash in Latin America," *The Economist*, November 30–December 6, 1996.

[2] The crime-reducing effect of income appeared robust to various regression specifications that controlled for preferences or tastes of different communities. For example, average family incomes tended to reduce crime even when taking into account the shares of the local young populations that were composed of African-Americans, divorced or single mothers, and immigrants.

[3] In the words of Fleisher (1966, 121), "in attempting to estimate the effect of income on delinquency, it is important to consider the effects of both normal family incomes and deviations from normal due to unemployment."

[4] Ehrlich (1981, 311–313) showed that the reduction in crime that follows the rehabilitation and/or incapacitation of past offenders is partially compensated by the entry or reentry of new offenders into the market, attracted by the temporary increase in the returns from crime that follows the departure of individual offenders. The author demonstrates that while the aggregate response of the supply of offenses to the removal of past offenders—through incapacitation or rehabilitation—decreases with the elasticity of this function (with respect to the return from offenses), the efficacy of general deterrence increases with this elasticity.

[5] The crime rate is the number of crimes over population, while the arrest (or conviction) rate is the number of arrests (convictions) over the number of reported crimes. Therefore, it is possible that a negative relationship may exist between these two variables simply because underreporting would produce a downward bias in the crime rate, while raising the arrest (conviction) rate. However, the relationship between these variables may be more complex, because the number of arrests (convictions) also depends on the number of reported crimes.

[6] For a comprehensive survey of models of criminal behavior, see Schmidt and Witte (1984, 165–182).

[7] Lower-case letters represent the variables related to a particular individual (not necessarily a representative individual in society). Upper-case letters represent society's averages for the respective variables.

[8] Drug possession crime rates and the lagged values of the intentional homicide and robbery rates were also used as explanatory variables. "Total" homicide statistics were collected for this project, but were not used in the econometric analysis because we feared that this broader definition of "homicide" was subject to more definition differences across countries than "intentional" homicide.

[9] The homicide rates for Argentina, Brazil, Colombia, Mexico, and Venezuela were constructed from data provided by the Health Situation Analysis Program of the Division of Health and Human Development, Pan-American Health Organization, from the PAHO Technical Information System. This source provided us with data on the annual number of deaths attributed to homicides, which come from national vital statistics systems.

[10] Most of the data was provided by Loayza et al. (1998). For some countries not covered by these authors, however, the conversion factors were constructed on the basis of information from World Bank databases.

[11] We followed, in this respect, the suggestion of Deininger and Squire (1996, 582) of adding to the indices based on expenditure the average difference of 6.6 between expenditure-based and income-based coefficients.

[12] "Net" enrollment rates (the fraction of people of secondary-school age who are enrolled in secondary school) are not available for a large number of developing countries.

[13] An indication that the negative relationship between homicide and conviction rates may be partially spurious is given by the suspicious jumps in the fit of the regression when the conviction rate is included as an explanatory variable.

[14] We do not include the homicide conviction rate in the core regression for two reasons; first, the variables to be examined are likely to also proxy for the strength of the police and judicial system; and second, the inclusion of the conviction rate reduces the sample size of the estimated regression by about 25%.

[15] We also ran regressions that included an index of the coverage of firearm regulations and the share of national population encompassed by males of 15–29 years of age as explanatory variables—see Table A1 for a description of these variables. However, the results showed that these variables were not significant determinants of intentional homicide rates. In addition, we collected information regarding the incidence of firearms and alcohol consumption in a group of countries, but this data was only available for a small group of countries, the regressions contained only 18 countries, and the coefficients of these variables were also statistically insignificant.

[16] For a concise presentation of the GMM estimator addressed to a general audience, see the appendix of Easterly, Loayza, and Montiel (1997) and chapter 8 of Baltagi (1995).

[17] We are grateful to Stephen Bond for providing us with a program to apply his and Arellano's estimator to an unbalanced panel data set.

[18] The absolute level of poverty (usually measured as the percentage of people below a certain level of income) is determined by the national income and its pattern of distribution. Hence, when GDP grows, while holding the Gini index constant, the abolute level of poverty declines.

[19] It must be noted that the differences between the results found in the levels and differences specifications are not solely the result of controlling for country-specific effects, for in the latter case the sample size is much smaller than in the former.

[20] The fact that the coefficient on secondary enrollment remains positive even after accounting for criminal inertia and country-specific effects makes it unlikely that this controversial coefficient sign is due to the omission of some relevant variable in the homicide rate regression.

[21] The remarkable similarity between the homicide and robbery regression results gives credence to our interpretation of the homicide rate as a relatively broad proxy for criminal behavior.

REFERENCES

Alonso-Borrego, C., and M. Arellano. 1996. "Symmetrically Normalised Instrumental Variable Estimation Using Panel Data." CEMFI Working Paper No. 9612, September.

Anderson, T.W., and C. Hsiao. 1981. "Estimation of Dynamic Models with Error Components." *Journal of the American Statistical Association* 76: 598–606.

Arellano, M., and O. Bover. 1995. "Another Look at the Instrumental-Variable Estimation of Error-Components Models." *Journal of Econometrics* 68: 29–52.

Arellano, Manuel, and Stephen Bond. 1991. "Estimation of Dynamic Models with Error Components." *Journal of the American Statistical Association* 76: 598–606.

Baltagi, Badi H. 1995. *Econometric Analysis of Panel Data.* New York: John Wiley & Sons.

Barro, Robert, and Jong-Wha Lee. 1996. "New Measures of Educational Attainment." Mimeographed. Department of Economics, Harvard Univeristy.

Becker, Gary S. 1993. "Nobel Lecture: The Economic Way of Looking at Behavior." *Journal of Political Economy* 101: 385–409.

Becker, Gary S. 1968. "Crime and Punishment: An Economic Approach." *Journal of Political Economy* 76: 169–217. Reprinted in *Chicago Studies in Political Economy*, edited by G.J. Stigler. Chicago and London: The University of Chicago Press, 1988.

Blundell, Richard, and Stephen Bond. 1997. "Initial Conditions and Moment Restrictions in Dynamic Panel Data Models." Discussion Papers in Economics 97-07, Department of Economics, University College London.

Caselli, Francesco, Gerardo Esquivel, and Fernando Lefort. 1996. "Reopening the Convergence Debate: A New Look at Cross-Country Growth Empirics. *Journal of Economic Growth.*

Chamberlain, Gary. 1984. "Panel Data." In *Handbook of Econometrics* Vol.2. Z. Griliches and M. D. Intriligator, eds.

Davis, Michael L. 1988. "Time and Punishment: An Intertemporal Model of Crime." *Journal of Political Economy* 96: 383–390.

Deninger, Klaus, and Lyn Squire. 1996. "A New Data Set Measuring Income Inequality." *The World Bank Economic Review* 10 (3): 565–592.

Easterly, William, and Ross Levine. 1997. "Africa's Growth Tragedy: Policies and Ethnic Divisions." *The Quarterly Journal of Economics* [November].

Easterly, William, Norman Loayza, and Peter Montiel. 1997. "Has Latin America's Post-Reform Growth Being Disappointing?" *Journal of International Economics* [Forthcoming].

Ehrlich, Isaac. 1973. "Participation in Illegitimate Activities: A Theoretical and Empirical Investigation." *Journal of Political Economy* 81: 521–565.

Ehrlich, Isaac. 1975a. "On the Relation between Education and Crime." In *Education, Income and Human Behavior,* edited by F.T. Juster. New York: McGraw-Hill.

Ehrlich, Isaac. 1975b. "The Deterrent Effect of Capital Punishment: A Question of Life and Death." *American Economic Review* [December]: 397–417.

Ehrlich, Isaac. 1981. "On the Usefulness of Controlling Individuals: An Economic Analysis of Rehabilitation, Incapacitation and Deterrence." *American Economic Review* 71(3): 307–322.

Ehrlich, Isaac. 1996. "Crime, Punishment, and the Market for Offenses." *Journal of Economic Perspectives* 10: 43–68.

Fleisher, Belton M. 1966. "The Effect of Income on Delinquency." *American Economic Review* 56: 118–137.

Glaeser, Edward L., Bruce Sacerdote, and Jose A. Scheinkman. 1996. "Crime and Social Interactions." *Quarterly Journal of Economics* 111: 507–548.

Griliches, Zvi, and Jerry Hausman. 1986. "Errors in Variables in Panel Data." *Journal of Econometrics* 31: 93–118.

Holtz-Eakin, Douglas, Whitney Newey, and Harvey S. Rosen. 1988. "Estimating Vector Autoregressions with Panel Data." *Econometrica* 56: 1371–1395.

Leung, Siu Fai. 1995. "Dynamic Deterrence Theory." *Economica* 62: 65–87.

Levitt, Steven D. 1995. "Why Do Increased Arrest Rates Appear to Reduce Crime: Deterrence, Incapacitation, or Measurement Error?" National Bureau of Economic Research Working Paper 5268, September, Cambridge, Massachusetts.

Loayza, Norman, Humberto Lopez, Klaus Schmidt-Hebbel, and Luis Serven. 1998. "A World Savings Database." Mimeographed, Policy Research Department, The World Bank, Washington, DC.

Newman, Graeme, and Bruce DiCristina. 1992. "Data Set of the 1st and 2nd United Nations World Crime Surveys." Mimeographed. School of Criminal Justice, State University of New York at Albany.

Posada, Carlos E. 1994. "Modelos económicos de la criminalidad y la posibilidad de una dinámica prolongada." *Planeación y desarrollo* 25: 217–225.

Sah, Raaj. 1991. "Social Osmosis and Patterns of Crime." *Journal of Political Economy* 99: 1272–1295.

Schmidt, Peter, and Ann D. Witte. 1984. *An Economic Analysis of Crime and Justice: Theory, Methods, and Applications.* New York: Academic Press, Inc.

Tauchen, Helen, and Ann D. Witte. 1994. "Work and Crime: An Exploration Using Panel Data." National Bureau of Economic Research Working Paper Series No. 4794, July.

Usher, Dan. 1993. "Education as a Deterrent to Crime." Queen's University, Institute for Economic Research, Discussion Paper No. 870, May.

World Bank. 1997. "Crime and Violence as Development Issues in Latin America and the Caribbean." Mimeographed, Office of the Chief Economist, Latin America and the Caribbean, The World Bank, Washington, DC.

WORLD BANK LATIN AMERICAN AND CARIBBEAN STUDIES

VIEWPOINT SERIES

Latin America after Mexico: Quickening the Pace
By Shahid Javed Burki and Sebastian Edwards

Poverty, Inequality, and Human Capital Development in Latin America, 1950–2025
By Juan Luis Londoño
Available in English and Spanish

Dismantling the Populist State: The Unfinished Revolution in Latin America and the Caribbean
By Shahid Javed Burki and Sebastian Edwards

Decentralization in Latin America: Learning through Experience
By George E. Peterson

Urban Poverty and Violence in Jamaica
By Caroline Moser and Jeremy Holland
Available in English and Spanish

Prospects and Challenges for the Caribbean
By Steven B.Webb

Black December: Banking Stability, the Mexican Crisis and its Effect on Argentina
By Valeriano García

The Long March: A Reform Agenda for Latin America and the Caribbean in the Next Decade
By Shahid Javed Burki and Guillermo E. Perry

Dealing with Public Risk in Private Infrastructure
Edited by Timothy Irwin, Michael Klein, Guillermo E. Perry and Mateen Thobani

Crime and Violence as Development Issues in Latin America and the Caribbean
By Robert L. Ayres

Financial Vulnerability, Spillover Effects, and Contagion: Lessons from the Asian Crises for Latin America
By Guillermo Perry and Daniel Lederman

Beyond the Washington Consensus: Institutions Matter
By Shahid Javed Burki and Guillermo Perry

Determinants of Crime Rates in Latin America and the World: An Empirical Assessment
By Pably Fajnzylber, Daniel Lederman and Norman Loayza

PROCEEDINGS SERIES

Currency Boards and External Shocks: How Much Pain, How Much Gain?
Edited by Guillermo Perry

Annual World Bank Conference on Development in Latin America and the Caribbean: 1995
The Challenges of Development
Edited by Shahid Javed Burki, Sebastian Edwards and Sri-Ram Aiyer

Annual World Bank Conference on Development in Latin America and the Caribbean: 1996
Poverty and Inequality
Edited by Shahid Javed Burki, Sri-Ram Aiyer, and Rudolf Hommes

Annual World Bank Conference on Development in Latin America and the Caribbean: 1997
Trade: Towards Open Regionalism
Edited by Shahid Javed Burki, Guillermo E. Perry and Sara Calvo

REGIONAL BOOKLETS AND BROCHURES

Summit of the Americas: Sustainable Cities in Latin America

The Burden of Poverty

¿Que significa para el Banco Mundial la reforma del estado?